A Bedtime Prayer

Now I lay me down to bed.
Great Spirit, bless my sleepy head.
As I journey through this night,
My silver cord will hold me tight.
Mother Earth and Father Sky,
Watch over me here where I lie,
For tomorrow I will greet the day
With love and joy and lots of play.

Also by Kristin Madden

Pagan Homeschooling:
A Guide to Adding Spirituality
to Your Child's Education

Pagan Parenting
(Revised Edition)

Spiritual, Magical, & Emotional
Development of the Child

 By Kristin Madden

Spilled Candy Books
Niceville, Florida USA

Pagan Parenting
Copyright 2000
Revised/expanded material, copyright 2004
By Kristin Madden

Published by: Spilled Candy Books,
Spilled Candy Publications
Post Office Box 5202
Niceville, FL 32578-5202
PaganParenting@spilledcandy.com
http://www.spilledcandy.com

ISBN: 1-892718-52-9 (trade paperback)
Revised edition
Printed in the United States of America
Library of Congress Card Catalog Number: 2004113289

Cover Photo: © Beth Conant
Author Photo: © Michael Foster aka Imajicka, http://www.twpt.com

For Karl
I love you with all that I am

Table of Contents

Chapter 1
Incarnation

The word *incarnate* means to have a physical body. Notice that this word doesn't mean to *be* a physical body. Clearly the definition implies that there is something that existed before the body and has taken on this new form. That something is the soul or spirit and the process of incarnation actually begins well before conception and continues beyond birth.

An understanding of this process allows us to determine how best to introduce certain religious or spiritual elements to our children—and when. It is also extremely valuable to keep in mind when creating a safe and healthy environment for children. The merging of spirit and body is gradual and mirrors the development of a child's physical, emotional, and mental capacities.

The spirit greatly influences the physical body, just as the body and life experiences influence the spirit. However, the energy systems that develop while we inhabit a physical body would not come into being without that body. It is a little like trying to decide whether the chicken or the egg came first.

Many people agree that the two systems begin to develop either at the moment of conception or at the point when the spirit decides to incarnate into a body that has already been conceived. From that point on, the spirit begins the process of integrating with the body. When the initial contact between spirit and developing body is made, an energetic link is established between the two. Some people see an energetic womb created around the embryo at this time; others see the beginnings of an aura.

During the course of pregnancy, the incoming spirit is generally present in the home and anywhere the mother-to-be goes. The spirit may show up at any point, even before conception. However, it is much more common that the child-to-be settles into the home during either the first or second trimester

Integration

As the baby's body develops, the link between spirit and body is strengthened. The spirit becomes more and more bound to the body. This dramatically affects the energy of body and spirit. No longer two separate systems, they merge to become something greater than the sum of their parts.

The moment when the spirit is fully integrated into the new body seems to vary. Some psychic healers have stated that this occurs instantaneously around the time of the quickening, or when the mother first feels the baby's movements. For many women, this is the case. However, for just as many other women, this process is a more gradual experience that may not be complete until the third trimester. And what's more—this process continues as the spirit-body system develops all the way through adolescence.

The spirit actually begins to merge with the energy field of the mother most commonly during the third trimester, although this can vary widely. Once this happens, the spirit becomes far less apparent as a separate being within the home. Psychically sensitive mothers may report experiencing a feeling of dualism, similar to that of the merging between person and spirit guide or God and Goddess among priests and priestesses. However, mothers and other family members are sometimes concerned that the spirit has left them and worry for the well-being of the unborn child.

As the energy field of the mother alters to accommodate the incoming spirit, her energy is dramatically altered. In addition to hormonal changes that are interrelated with these energetic changes, a pregnant woman must deal with an expanded energy field and opening chakra systems. As her energy, or aura, opens to merge with the incoming spirit, she is also open to the energies in her personal environment

Pre-Natal Communication

Communication with your baby-to-be may start earlier than you expect. Pre-conception communications are fairly common and not limited to the mother. A large number of fathers-to-be have contact with the incoming spirit both before conception and during pregnancy. While some of these contacts are simply the awareness that a spirit has chosen its intended parents, others have a definite intent. Sometimes the purpose of these contacts seems designed to bring future parents together. Other communications are more specific, often regarding a name for the baby.

Whether or not parents are aware of pre-conception contact, a great many experience dreams and other psychic messages during pregnancy. I had constant communication with our son during my pregnancy. He showed up when I was almost two months pregnant. Our contact began with a dream I had at about one-and-a-half months pregnant. I dreamed of "the baby." I could not tell if the baby was male or female, but it was blonde with blue eyes and full of light. This is the perfect description of our son. He has the most amazing blue eyes, though his hair gets darker every year.

I wrote in my journal: "We were out somewhere; it was approximately four months old. I was speaking to someone, and the baby spoke to me, helping me to explain something. I was amazed that it spoke like a very wise adult so early." I went on to have several more "speaking" dreams of our son. As time went on, the dreams became more involved and intense.

As my pregnancy progressed, so did my contact with Karl. He began to be a very distinct presence in our home at around four months of pregnancy. He was a huge and imposing mass of energy with a reddish tinge in our home. The color was very interesting particularly since my parents and I all saw it as red or reddish hair during dreaming. I generally saw it as strawberry-blonde. He has an incredibly strong life force that, even now, can manifest as a beautiful true red in his energy field.

In shamanic societies, it is common for the baby's name to be received by the mother, usually through dreams. If the parents do not receive a name for the child, the shaman will often go in search of the child's name through dreaming or shamanic journeying. In my family, a child's name is often received as a *knowing* during pregnancy.

In speaking with other metaphysical mothers, I have discovered that this is far more common than we may realize. Many mothers tell me that both they and their husbands or partners have received the names of their children well before delivery. This occurs in a variety of ways, including through dreams, visions, meditations, and simple intuitive feelings.

Like many new parents, my husband and I went around and around trying to decide on the right name for our son.

Karl made it all very easy for us. When I was between six and seven months pregnant, I began thinking of adding the name Carl to the list. We had never considered this name, but I had the distinct feeling this was the baby's idea. I was ambivalent toward the name but appreciated that it was also a family name on my mother's side.

One night around this same period of time, I was awakened in the middle of the night. As I walked through the hallway, I met the huge presence that had taken up residence in our home during my pregnancy. He was adamant that his name must be Karl and it must be spelled with a "K." There was no questioning his insistence and the fact that it was obviously very important to him. That was the end of that.

Psychic Effects of Pregnancy

Along with increased hormone levels, this can cause some women to be more emotional than usual. As is true when we menstruate, women are open to energies and emotions around us. We can easily pick up the feelings or thoughts of others without recognizing that these are not *our stuff.*

Because of this, it is important to keep your environment as consistently balanced and supportive as possible during pregnancy. Not only is the mother vulnerable to stress and unwanted energies, but the incoming spirit has not yet developed the necessary psychic shields to prevent the spiritual and physical damage that can result from an unhealthy atmosphere.

Many mothers will experience one or more kundalini risings during this time period. Throughout my second and third trimesters, and particularly during my last two months of pregnancy, the kundalini energy was very active along my spine. It was uncomfortable for me to lie down in certain positions because the energy moving up my spine was so intense.

This activation of kundalini energy accompanies the opening of the chakras and an increased receptivity to alternate realities. Many pregnant women often report that they are considerably more psychic or intuitive during pregnancy. This is beyond the connection to the unborn child, and carries over to all aspects of their lives. This receptivity also appears to increase as the pregnancy progresses.

Although I was always psychically sensitive, in my journal I recorded that I was becoming even more so throughout my pregnancy. There was a dramatic increase in telepathy and intuition during my third trimester. This coincided with Karl's integration into his physical body. It seemed that as I expanded to accommodate his energy field, I was also wide open to other people's thoughts and energies.

Not all women experience an increase in psychic awareness during pregnancy. Some women find quite the opposite is true for them. In pregnancies where the incoming spirit fully merges with its body at an early stage, the mother's energy tends to focus inward. Her energy is almost entirely involved in protecting the fetus and growing the new body.

Protection of both child and mother is another common reason for a shutting down of psychic awareness during pregnancy. My friend Kethry is very aware that she had been pregnant with the spirit of one of her daughters and miscarried. Several months later, she became pregnant with her daughter-to-be again. She shut herself down psychically in order to protect both herself and her baby from another miscarriage.

To make matters worse, when she was in California during a serious earthquake, Kethry felt her psychic shields shatter and effectively buffered herself and her unborn child by shutting down completely. This psychic buffering in not uncommon among pregnant women, especially in times of crisis. Kethry notes that her second daughter began the process of unwinding her from her "cocoon."

Many women experience the integration of the incoming spirit during the early months of pregnancy. But it appears that the majority of pregnant mothers feel this during the third trimester. Some women became very afraid when they noticed the lack of that external spirit. Some were frantic that something had gone wrong with the pregnancy. A few women even went in for an additional medical examination to be sure the baby was still alive.

Seven days before the birth of our son, I wrote in my journal that he had been hanging around a lot less recently and seemed to be more in his own body. It was an unusual feeling. I went from having a constant companion outside to carrying a being-in-transition within my body. As he integrated into his body, his energy was completely focused on becoming that new person.

Karl had an enormous energy field when he showed up at our house. It seemed to be difficult for him to fully compact himself into that tiny body. It is interesting to note that toward the end of that time period, my uterus grew twice the normal rate in one month. My doctors were concerned enough about this growth spurt that they had me go through the full eight-hour test for gestational diabetes, which might explain an unusual increase in the size of the baby. We also got to see another ultrasound of him. All tests were normal. Karl had decided that it was time to move in.

Pre-Natal Attunement

During pregnancy and early infancy, children respond best to sensory input and symbolic images. They are not yet ready for the language-based communication that is the norm in this reality. Thanks to ultrasound, we now have scientific evidence that babies as young as seven weeks react to external stimuli.

Many people from scientists to parents-to-be have experimented with reading stories or playing music to babies *in utero*. My husband and I did the same. In the beginning of my third trimester, my husband sang and spoke to our son through my belly. Our baby definitely moved in response to Dave's voice. When Dave switched sides, Karl moved toward his voice. When Dave sang, Karl squirmed.

Guided imagery, music, and voice are frequently used to stimulate an unborn child early in the pregnancy. Many people today use these methods as an early "educational" tool to give their children a step up academically. But I find them to be great tools for strengthening the energetic connections parents have with their children and in developing intuitive abilities.

I suggest simply seeking attunement with your unborn child at first, especially if you are early in your pregnancy. Some books direct parents seemingly to quiz the unborn baby with psychic games. Certainly, these tests can be beneficial in developing your own intuition. However, unless the baby is far enough along for you to ask it to kick or move as answer, there is no easy way to be sure whether the images you are receiving are from the baby or your own intuition.

Furthermore, we are the ones who need validation for "extra-sensory" perception. These incoming beings may find these games amusing or play along for our benefit, but they need no training to communicate outside everyday physical reality. It is the everyday physical reality that they will need to relearn. What will benefit everyone most is the fostering of an early relationship built on love and trust. The ability to use non-physical senses can only strengthen that relationship and make communication more effective, throughout the lives of all involved.

With that in mind, I have outlined several exercises and guided visualizations for use during pregnancy. These need not be limited to the pregnant woman, but I do recommend that anyone else planning to use these exercises let the mother-to-be know before beginning. If she is unaware that someone is working with the child within her, she may be unnerved or even frightened at the additional presence or energy changes that may occur. If the child-to-be is present within your home but not yet integrated into the body, you may also wish to use your own practice of meditation or shamanic journeying to communicate with this being.

Attunement to the baby in the womb

Initially to be done in a safe space where you will be undisturbed for at least one hour. Once a psychic relationship begins to develop, this may be done anywhere and anytime. It is beneficial to use during times of stress for mother or child, or in uncomfortable surroundings.

If you would like to do this exercise with a partner, choose one of you to lead the exercise with spoken directions or tape record it to play back during the meditation. Hold hands or sit very close to one another throughout the exercise.

Make yourself very comfortable. Take care of any bathroom or food needs ahead of time. Light some incense or candles. Cast a Circle or simply call in the Spirits of the directions, if you feel more comfortable this way.

Take a deep breath and relax. Count yourself down from ten to one, stopping periodically to remind yourself to take a deep breath and go deeper. Visualize a bubble forming, just before your face. Blow all your fears, stresses, irritations—any negative energies you may be carrying around—into this bubble. Watch the bubble grow and begin to rise. Blow the last of these energies into the bubble and watch as it flies off toward the sun, carrying these things away from you. Feel very centered and relaxed.

Feel the energy of the Earth, flowing up through the soles of your feet (or the base of your spine if you are seated on the floor). Feel and visualize this light filling you completely. It flows out your pores and your eyes and out through the top of your head.

Become aware of the energy of the Universe flowing into you through the top of your head and filling your body. Feel and visualize this light filling you completely. It flows out your pores and your eyes and down through the soles of your feet (or the base of your spine).

Visualize and feel these energies flowing through you at the same time. See them as balanced and centering you. You are energized and revitalized.

Now, turn your attention inward to your womb. Be aware of any sensations or images that come to mind. Send a gentle stream of love and peacefulness to the child within you. Visualize an image of you, smiling and happy with this child in your life. If you are practicing this with a partner, both of you should visualize the same images together. Follow the image of mother with an image of the partner.

As you progress with this exercise and as your pregnancy progresses, you may choose to use this exercise to introduce your child to the rest of the family. They do not need to be present, only in your mental images. You may also use this exercise to learn more about your child by being very aware of images or thoughts and by asking questions. Feel free to experiment and discover what works best for you.

Dreaming Your Baby #1

I recommend keeping a pen and paper beside your bed so that you may write down your dreams as soon as you wake up. Keep in mind that you may awaken during the night and should write it down before falling back to sleep.

As you lie down to go to sleep, count yourself down from ten to one, stopping periodically to remind yourself to take a deep breath and go deeper. If you find you are still tense from the day, count down again from ten to one. When you are very relaxed and nearing sleep, tell yourself with belief and intent that you will meet with your unborn child tonight during dreaming *and* that you will remember it upon awakening.

Turn your attention to the child in your womb. If you are not the mother, focus your attention on your image of the baby and continue as directed. Visualize your intention to meet with this being in a dream that night and send it with the feel of a question. Be specific that you are asking the child to meet you in a dream.

Allow yourself to fall asleep.

Dreaming Your Baby #2

Before going to sleep, count yourself down from ten to one as usual. Once you are relaxed and centered, take up a fresh glass of water between both hands and hold it just above eye level. With eyes closed, visualize this water filling with your intention to meet your child during dreaming. State specifically that you will remember the dream(s) upon awakening and then drink the water.

Allow yourself to fall asleep.

*A pregnant mom may want to use a half or a quarter of a glass of water to prevent a late-night bathroom run.

Meeting Your Child's Spirit Guides

Allow at least one hour when you will not be disturbed. This exercise can also be done through either of the above dreaming techniques.

Make yourself very comfortable. Take care of any bathroom or other needs ahead of time. Light some incense or candles. Cast a Circle or call in the Spirits of the directions, if you feel more comfortable this way.

Imagine that you are in your favorite place of relaxation. This may be a real or imagined place, but it should be somewhere that you feel perfectly safe and comfortable.

Call upon your own spirit guides to join you in this journey to meet the guides of your child. Be aware of any images or thoughts, as well as what guides show up. It may help to imagine a doorway or an elevator for your guides to use as an entryway, if they choose.

Speak with your guides and let them know exactly what your intentions are during this journey. Ask their guidance, protection, and assistance.

Invite your child's guides to join you in this place. It may help to imagine a doorway or an elevator for your guides to use as an entryway, if they choose. Be aware of any images or thoughts, as well as what beings may show up.

When you meet with a being, ask for confirmation that this is one of the guides of this child. You may receive confirmation as a feeling or as an indication from your guides or the being in question.

Take a good look at this being and ask who it is (or what it is). Accept whatever is given in response. Ask any questions you may have regarding this child or your relationship with this child.

You may choose to ask what you can do to help this child succeed with the current life plan or about a past-life connection. You may also want to ask for their assistance in creating a safe, healthy pregnancy and delivery for both you and your child. Ask whatever you feel compelled to and accept whatever is given in response.

Thank this being (or beings) for meeting with you. Tell them of your love for this child and that you are open to them in any way that may benefit this child. Say your goodbyes and thank them once more.

You may wish to review this experience with your own guides before returning to everyday reality.

If you used a countdown, count yourself back up from one to ten. If you are using a tape, allow the drumming to return you to this reality.

One last note, before we move on to the child after birth: It is a good idea to keep a journal of these exercises as well as any dreams or other experiences you have. This is an excellent way to record your experiences and your development on these levels of being. It can be invaluable in determining your personal symbolism as well as honing your accuracy. You may wish to keep separate journals for each child: to be given to them along with other baby books when they grow up.

Chapter 2
Development of
Energy Systems

Along with the physical body, the human energy system develops as a child grows. The two are vitally interconnected and their development mirrors each other. An understanding of this development can be extremely beneficial for the pagan parent, not only when working on magic but also during everyday activities. Our energy systems influence and are influenced by everything in our environment: mental, physical, emotional, and spiritual.

When a child is born, all of its spiritual energy is fully integrated into the body. This energy begins to merge with the physical energy starting at the head and moving down through the body. The fontanels, which are so soft and must be protected in a baby's head, are the physical manifestation of the wide-open crown chakra. As a child grows and becomes more grounded in the body, the root chakra opens up and the crown chakra closes down a bit, to balance the other energy centers.

Effects of Unhealthy Environments

Both violence and neglect have the potential to damage the chakras of both children and adults and cause blockages or soul loss. Juvenile crime and teen pregnancies are frequently the result of generations of wounded souls, reacting out of their own pain and numbness. These children are no longer able to feel a connection to their expanded selves, other beings, or the natural world. As a result, respect and honor have no meaning.

Children know instinctively to go to a trusted person for comfort and protection from these influences. When we hold our children, we are shielding them with our energy fields; much like a mother does when still pregnant with her child. We provide the buffers they need until they develop their own. When a child has no buffers, the wounding can be extreme.

I have known children who were raised in extremely violent and non-nurturing environments. Some of these children saw loved ones killed before their eyes when they were very young. Most of these children had no adults to love or shield them. By the time their own shields developed, several of these children no longer really needed them. They learned to shut down completely all but those chakras essential for physical survival.

Many of these children have grown up to be wonderful people. They love children and several of them now work toward global protection of children. But I can still see the intense need for approval and love whenever I am with them.

Many of them also retain another side with tough outer shell that can be impenetrable if they feel the slightest threat. They often react to perceived threats by lashing out and shutting down. These individuals have some of the strongest self-protective mechanisms I have ever seen. And they remind me that too many of the children in the world today have developed similar measures to protect themselves from the continual assault on their developing systems.

Very strong emotions, such as rage, uncontrolled lust, and deep depression within a child's environment can shock a young child's energy systems, much like physical trauma shocks the body. Physical shock jars the body. It can lead to a depressed physical condition.

Physical shock causes necessary blood flow to be withdrawn from the extremities. This survival mechanism is designed to sacrifice "non-essential" body parts to prevent the death of the organism. Shock may even shut down physical systems, leading to death if untreated. Energetic shock is very similar and can directly affect physical, mental, and emotional behavior.

Children who are exposed to this type of environment have no way to filter these energies. They cannot really understand these emotions. Yet they receive them with full force and must deal with them in some way. Some children are fairly good at automatically grounding some of this energy out, if it is not continual.

However, many children cannot handle this influx of extreme adult energy. They react with nightmares, insecurities, hostility, and other behavioral problems that are the result of shocked and damaged chakras. From a shamanic point of view, these children experience soul fragmentation. They may also exhibit physical problems in the area where the damage to the energy field has occurred.

With these cautions in mind, let's move on to the stages of physical and energetic development. Each of these stages is unique and the magical or psychic work you include your children in should be based on their specific stages. Of course, each child is an individual and their development may not match up with these stages according to their physical age. But as an observant and loving parent, you will be able to tell what stage is appropriate for your children .

Infants

Because the spirit takes time to merge with the physical body, infants are not fully connected to this reality. They are still very open to other dimensions and usually retain memories of past lives.

As I said in the introduction, infants may continue to be in contact with friends and relatives from the past, either from past lives or between lives. It can sometimes be difficult for them to let go of these relationships. As parents, we need to be understanding of this, even as we encourage the transfer of these emotional bonds to us.

The heightened sensitivity that many pregnant and new mothers experience can be attributed both to the gradual process that separates the mother's energy from the child's and to the development of an independent energy system in the newborn.

Many new parents, not just mothers, experience a continuing Oneness with their newborns. Some people have experienced a physical feeling of inhabiting the body of the newborn: seeing through her eyes or a sudden snapping back into the parent's body when they realize their perspective of a baby's stretch is from the baby's body.

I experienced these types of perspective shifts when my son was born. I also experienced a series of popping sounds as our energy separated or as we returned to this reality from inter-dimensional journeys. These were like the sound a balloon makes when it breaks, and they always shocked me quickly back into this reality and my own body. Once the separation of our energy fields was complete, the popping stopped.

When children are very young, a great deal of their parents' personal energy flows into them through this energy umbilical cord. This parental energy supports the development of their energy systems and protects them from external influences.

As they grow and their energy systems stabilize, they no longer need such an intense connection to their parents, and the cord fades a bit.

As any new parent will tell you, infants sleep much of the time, waking mainly for food and diaper changes. During this sleep time, the astral body, or what many shamans refer to as the free soul, occupies the higher chakras and their associated energy bodies. In a way, babies are half-in and half-out of the physical body during infancy.

Some infants do seem to have lost their conscious awareness in the womb and are truly re-awakening as new beings in the physical world. However, many infants at this time struggle not only to release inter-dimensional loved ones, but also to separate who they were in past incarnations from the current life. Some may resist being limited once more by a physical body; or they may have changed their minds about this incarnation. Any of these issues may result in illness, extreme colic, or disease.

While the free soul handles inter-dimensional issues, the body soul (which is often associated with the lower chakras) is occupied with building the physical body and grounding the rest of the energy to the physical plane. The spinning of the chakras plays an important part in keeping the physical and energy systems intact.

This can be a difficult process as the spirit attempts to fit its entire energy field into a very small infant's body. As I wrote earlier, our son had an enormous energy field when he arrived at our home. He had some difficulty integrating and grounding all this energy into his physical body. The lower chakra difficulties manifested as digestive problems that he grew out of as soon as he fully integrated into his body.

As infants grow, they begin to recognize and respond to their own names. Children begin to learn the language of their family and attempt to communicate in this way. They begin to show signs of thinking and will experiment with the things in their surroundings as they learn how this world works. All of this coincides with the separation of energy fields and the spirit's integration into the physical body.

With each new milestone, or each experiment and change in awareness, infant's auras and chakras become slightly more defined. As they focus on a new toy or begin to find a partially hidden object, their auras seem to sharpen and color more brightly. Colors are deepened or new colors are added with each new experience. The aura stretches toward the objects they focus on.

Babies tend to have pastel auras. It is interesting that our society often views pastels as baby colors. These are the colors that most infant clothes come in. In fact, it can be difficult to find baby gifts in any colors other than white and pastels. People who can see chakras find that infants' chakras are softer and less rigid than those of adults.

An adult chakra is relatively fixed. It occupies a specific place in the body and has a definite shape. The chakras of the infant and young child reflect their greater connection to the world of Spirit and their relative lack of defining belief systems. As children grow and learn more of our world, their energy systems become more fixed within an adult shape.

While the chakras are developing, the energy field remains open to external influences. This is yet another reason to maintain a healthy and honest environment around our children. They can and do pick up the psychic and emotional atmosphere of the family, even repressed or hidden issues.

In general, infants cannot be "trained." They can be exposed to elements of the family religion and/or spirituality. This is the best way for children to grow up feeling these ways are natural and normal. However, it is very important that infants not be exposed to potentially dangerous or extreme magic. It is sufficient for them to attend holiday celebrations, Naming ceremonies, or other celebratory rituals that do not include strong magical forces.

Toddlers

As babies develop into toddlers, they begin to separate even more from their parents. Toddlers have reached the point where their stuff is "Mine." This often accompanies the beginnings of imaginative play. By this time, they are fairly well integrated into their bodies and their lower chakras are beginning to develop. Toddlers now understand that they are individual beings. As a result, they begin to assign ownership to people, animals, and things.

Toddlers go through a constant struggle between being an individual with a defined personal auric field and being psychically connected to other life forms, particularly their parents. They are testing the waters of individuality. Sometimes your two-year-old will amaze you as she shares and offers certain toys to a playmate. Five minutes later, you may hear screaming because she decided that toy is hers, even if she does not want to play with it.

Remember how the auras of infants stretched out toward the things they focused on? This is taken to a new level in the toddler years. That stretching continues, but filaments of the child's energy field surround anything (or anyone) they decide belongs to them. These filaments remain attached to these things, becoming a part of their energy fields. These are the beginnings of the energy cords that bond us to the people and things in our lives.

Toddlers are very similar to infants in the types of energies they must be protected from. Toddlers gain the most benefit from holiday celebrations and they tend to enjoy these immensely. This is also the age where bedtime prayers and special stories make a big impact. Little ones (who are past the point of putting everything in their mouths) love to collect stones and feathers and amulets. Be warned that most wild bird feathers are illegal. This does not merely apply to birds of prey or endangered species. Domestic bird feathers, like turkey or goose, are wonderful beginning ritual tools for toddlers.

The toddler age is the time to introduce the concepts of fairies or angels and other helping spirits, respect for all life, and the fact that the Earth itself is alive, too. This is a very active age, with a very short attention span. As a result, physically active rituals and exercises may be essential. Beginning yoga, dances, songs, and easy games are favorites among children at this age. Toddlers also respond very well to introductory ritual elements, such as smudging, charging liquids, and saying thank-you to the Great Spirit/God/Goddess or Spirits of the directions.

Daycare

The natural separation that begins in the toddler years and continues through adolescence is often forced upon children who enter a full-time daycare situation as infants and toddlers. Many young children will develop similar energetic bonds to their daycare teachers as they do to their parents. A thin energetic cord can often be observed between these children and their teacher or teachers.

These children can become very upset if their usual teacher is out sick or moves on to another job. Children may experience a separation anxiety that has been transferred from the parents or added to the usual daycare teacher. Slightly older children, particularly toddlers, may feel betrayed or abandoned if their teacher is seen working with children in another room.

In some cases, children are unable to form the necessary energetic bonds with a teacher. When the parent leaves, these children not only lose a familiar buffer from outside influences, but they may feel a tearing or stretching of the cord that binds them to their parent. Children who are beginning to see themselves as individuals may find this absolute independence from the influence of their parents to be terrifying.

These are those children who cry all day long, act out in destructive behaviors, or isolate themselves and shut down their emotional reactions. A strong and healthy family relationship can be vital in preventing this from developing, or easing these effects, with sensitive children.

The truth is that our energetic bonds to our children are never really broken, nor do they disappear as we get farther physically from our children. But at a young age, so much of our energy is still flowing into our children and they feel it when our attention is focused elsewhere. When they are not present to regain our attention physically, they can feel abandoned.

I do not include this to make any parent feel bad about using a daycare center. Daycare is a necessary and often beneficial fact of modern life. This is merely what I (and others) have observed. I include it so parents can recognize these issues if they arise and handle them appropriately. If you have noticed changes in your children's behavior, perhaps they need some additional time at home while you focus solely on them. They may need more physical contact or your undivided attention as they recount the events of the day.

Our son and I have conjunct Moons in Pisces, which creates an intense and unavoidable psychic and emotional bond. When he was in daycare a couple of days a week, he needed some additional Mommy-time when he came home. Sometimes, all it took was a few extra hugs; other days he needed some extended time and physical contact with me.

Some children need more recharging and comfort from a parent's energy field than others do. At this young age, it is counter-productive to pressure our children to toughen up. It is far more beneficial to their developing energy systems, as well as their emotional and psychological well-being, to give them the comfort and support they require, within reason. Because as we all know—parents need downtime, too.

Children

When children are approximately seven years old, filters begin to form over their chakras. These filters buffer incoming energy. They are the first step in the child's ability to protect themselves energetically. As we grow up, our filters strengthen.

Children at these ages no longer need constant adult buffers. They have developed distinct personal energy fields. As their chakra filters form, children feel safer away from their parents. They may spend more time with friends and outside of their own homes. They may even get involved in extra-curricular activities at this point. Their energy fields are more protected and they are comfortable exploring their individuality.

By this age, children have learned much of what is acceptable in society. In our society, they are often involved in fitting in with other children, play, and television. Depending on their particular culture, children may begin to block psychic awareness at this age. Those other senses we all possess tend to be pushed into the realm of the unconscious in modern, mainstream families.

This is the perfect age to begin to encourage your children to use these abilities, before they are completely blocked. In many pagan traditions, children are dedicated to the path of their parents at this age and may begin to participate in some ritual workings, other than holiday celebrations. The key to this type of training is to keep it fun, though serious, and not allow it to evolve into work for the child.

Some children find their own paths around this age and dedicate to their own Gods. Our son decided that he was Heathen a little after his eighth birthday. He (and many people) considers this to be a specific pagan path, focusing on the Old Gods of the Norse tradition. Before this, he set out to learn all he could about the Norse pantheon, mythology, and the history of the Vikings. A few months after he turned eight, he got himself a Thor's hammer, made a drum bearing runic inscriptions, created a webpage on my site devoted to Thor, and dedicated himself to the Heathen path. This is not our path, but we continue to do all we can to help him learn more and participate in Norse rituals.

As children progress academically and adapt to modern technological society, their mental chakras begin to develop. Children learn to think and use their mental capacities from a very young age in a technological culture. Not only does this mental development allow for increased complexity in thought and learning, but it also provides fodder for active young imaginations.

Children at these ages are masters at make-believe. They truly seem to create whatever it is that they are pretending. The influx of mental energy at this point only adds to their creative abilities. This also contributes to the productivity of any spiritual training process.

Once the chakra filters have begun to form, children may participate in more directed training. It is vital that you not only keep this training fun, but that you also refrain from pushing children to do anything they strongly prefer not to.

At this age, the ever-present make-believe focus may be used to the child's advantage. Visualization games and exercises are ideal for helping children gain access to their inner selves as well as helping them to develop stronger connections with helping spirits.

Even young school age children will excel at most of the games and exercises in this book. They may love to create their own altars and they take the initiative in many holiday celebrations. While some people have had success meditating with children as young as three, it is normally most productive beginning in the early school years. Keep in mind the attention span of each individual child as you meditate along with her. As long as you allow for giggle fits on occasion, it can be a truly wonderful practice to share with your children.

As children grow, so does their ability to focus for extended periods of time. Their abilities to ground and protect themselves also increase dramatically over the school-age years. Depending on the individual child, more focused meditations and simple rituals may be introduced. Participating in Moon rituals and assuming roles in holiday celebrations increase a child's independence and self-confidence. Children may take an interest in a specific Deity or path. This should be encouraged whenever possible. Assist them in creating ritual clothing or tools.

Teens

Eventually your child reaches puberty and you wonder where your little boy or girl went. Some parents feel they don't even know their children and cannot understand them at this age. The truth is that sometimes your children don't know themselves either. A tremendous amount of change is occurring on all levels of being throughout adolescence. It can be a challenge for all involved just to get through it.

Hormonal changes are directly related to spiritual changes. In fact, all physical events are preceded by a spiritual cause. With regard to puberty and the teenage years, the hormonal imbalances that make kids and their parents so crazy are related to another period of flux in the personal energy field.

Popularity and fitting in may become even more important as our kids reach puberty. Suddenly, the opposite sex (for most teenagers) is the most important thing in the world. They cannot stop thinking about their appearance, whether they are cool enough, if they hang out with the right crowd, and if that special someone likes them back. They seem to make a big deal out of everything and even a hair out of place is treated with absolute horror.

Teenagers become like toddlers once more, except to a much more complex degree. What may seem trivial to an adult is a matter of huge importance to a teen. Losing a boyfriend or girlfriend is accorded a similar reaction to that of the toddler whose favorite toy is taken by a playmate.

Those filaments that attached the toddler to the people and things he decided were his are still around. And they still get attached to people and things that are "owned." This is not something that most people grow out of. To some extent, we all have these filaments connecting us to our people and our stuff. Adults often react with similar intensity when we lose a job or return to a car in a parking lot to find it broken into.

With all the spiritual and physical changes going on in the body of an adolescent, the loss of a person or thing of importance can cause a very real wound in the personal energy field. An auric hole is opened up whenever one of these cords is torn free. This is particularly true when it comes to relationships with romantic interests and the often-public nature of teenage relationships.

Once again, children are struggling with individuality and their connections to others. This time, the individuality is more about being somewhere between child and adult, as well as establishing one's Self in relation to peers. The chakras are fairly well defined. But this is not the time to get inexperienced children deeply involved in magical or psychic work. While they are connecting and testing their places within the community of other teens, they tend to be highly open on an emotional level. They frequently waver between experiencing wide-open heart chakras (and sometimes lower chakras) and shutting down in self-defense.

Most teens do not have the control over their emotions and their energy systems to handle the influence of everything they may encounter on a magical or psychic level. They may be ready for more advanced work, but they are still children. They continue to need the guidance and protection of a parent or guardian.

And so, it is with these stages of development in mind that we will proceed with this book. Keep in mind that there are no hard and fast rules and that the development of the individual may vary slightly from what I have discussed here. The best way to know when your child is ready for something new is to get to know your child and develop your own intuition. As parents, this is a relatively easy task since we are already connected to them on a psychic level.

Chapter 3
Innate Psychic Abilities

Most pagans appreciate that psychic abilities are a natural part of the human condition. We all possess these abilities to some degree and use them at a very early age. It is only through the indoctrination of limiting beliefs and the total immersion in this reality that we block our psychic, or extra-physical, perception.

We know that children begin this incarnation more connected to the other dimensions than this one. We also know that as we grow, our focus shifts to a three-dimensional perception, altering our experience. But what does this mean in terms of psychic or magical abilities?

Generally speaking, these "extra" senses and levels of being are just like the physical in that they are usable to the extent that we develop them. They can be compared to an unused muscle that gets stronger and more flexible with use. It is also true that our individual talents may differ.

For example, a great baseball player is not necessarily a great violinist, although she may be. Willow may be fantastic at entering deep trances and returning with accurate and pertinent information. Shadowhawk, on the other hand, may struggle with trance but may be very telepathic in everyday life. It is important to keep this in mind when working within a specific path or with a certain area of psychic ability.

Few of us are exceptionally talented in every area of life. I was a good pilot, a fair swimmer, and really bad at throwing a football. Such is life this time around, and I work within my talents. This does not mean that I do not have a lot of fun playing with the areas where I am less talented. But to put pressure on oneself to achieve greatness in all areas, or perfection in any one area at all times, is counter-productive.

Set realistic goals for yourself and your children. Do your best to laugh at your mistakes and play with your successes. Use each experience as an opportunity for growth and learning. Support each other in the process. I strongly suggest that you work to develop your own way of seeing.

Seeing and *sight* are generic terms used to describe the ways in which we receive telepathic, prophetic, or Otherworldly information and communications. Literally, it means the perception of visions or the ability to perceive spirits. But our perception of these things differs. Just as we differ in this reality between being predominantly visual, auditory, or sensory, these tendencies carry over into the psychic realms.

One person may receive visions or see spirits, almost as if with his physical eyes. Another individual may hear voices resulting from a telepathic link. She may hear voices or other sounds indicating the presence of spirits or an overlap of realities.

Still another may perceive these things with some type of feeling. These feelings may be physical sensations, such as a chill or tingling, or they may be simply a *knowing*. When we receive communications or impressions in this way, we just know what the spirit wants to communicate, that there is someone "else" present, or what another person is thinking or feeling. The key is to determine in what area your strengths lie and to separate your own stuff from that of others.

The goal, whatever it may be, is a wonderful thing to set one's sights on. But the process, the journey, is really the place to be. Being present, *in the now*, is the only place we really can be. Living in the future or the past is an avoidance tactic. So I invite you all to become explorers rather than seekers.

Our children are great explorers and we can learn a great deal from them. Rather than seeking and looking for something "out there" that we feel is missing, children explore what is present right now. Fully experience the place you are in and the growth potential you are presented with each day. In this way, you become a shining example for your children and all those around you.

The Shadow Side

Many pagans work intensively with their shadow sides. The shadow side is that place within each of us where we hide all of our weaknesses, fears, embarrassments, as well as our hidden strengths. This is that dark place, deep within, where we keep all those aspects of Self that we do not want to acknowledge and do not want other people to know are a part of us. Unfortunately, repressing and denying these sides does not make them go away. Quite the opposite, it gives them even more power over our lives.

These repressed aspects become our unknown urges and the uncontrolled reactions. We may experience them as behavior or feelings that we have no control over. These aspects refuse to be denied and will use any opportunity to get us to face them. They manifest in all aspects of our lives; attracting situations that may be used as opportunities for growth. Often these situations are difficult and we cannot understand where they came from. We can move out of town, dump our current relationships, and switch jobs, but those uncomfortable patterns follow us everywhere.

Why do I bring this up in a book on pagan parenting?

For two very important reasons. The child who learns at an early age to know her Self and to act with wisdom, rather than react from ignorance, grows up to be a much happier and healthier adult. These are the children who will have the power to re-create our society and bring us into balance once again. As parents, an understanding of these issues allows us to be better guides for our children. The other reason may not be so obvious.

Anyone who works on a psychic level without clearing personal shadow issues will have difficulty seeing clearly and accurately. As I said, the shadow side will show up in all aspects of our lives. This includes all levels of being. Repressed issues or memories can alter our perception on all levels.

These issues may show up (on all levels) as external beings or forces. Many of the frightening images that are encountered during dreaming and the early stages of trance work are simply the projection of our inner selves. These can also manifest in the people and situations around us.

It is for these reasons that I encourage people to maintain a balance between inner work, such as meditation and shamanic journeying, and outer work, like magic and ritual. As parents, it is our responsibility to guide and protect our children. This includes getting to know our Selves. When considering involving children in any type of metaphysical working, we need to make our decisions based on what is best for their total soul growth. Imbalance does not lead to healthy development. Self-knowledge leads to true wisdom and power.

With all that said, let's get on with learning to develop our own talents (and of course, those of our children) and to use them for our greatest benefit. I have separated what one might term "psychic" abilities into subsections of this chapter. Each subsection contains a description of the ability and exercises or games that will help in developing that strength. Parents should be encouraged to play along with children. Make it a family affair and have fun with it.

Also, be aware of what areas your children prefer and encourage them to develop those areas. Areas in which they are ambivalent or dislike should not be pushed. They may just have no interest in these areas, or perhaps their intuition tells them that their strengths lie in other areas. Perhaps they are just not ready for these areas yet. Whatever the reason, we do not want to create blocks or resistance to these areas. Go with the flow, as they say.

Breathing

Breathing is certainly an innate ability. We all breathe, but why discuss it in this type of book? Because breathing has a surprising power to affect our abilities to remain focused, emotionally stable, and to assist us in attaining trance states.

The impact of the body on the breath—and the breath on the body—is clear during an emotional outburst. When we are frightened or very upset, we begin to breathe more quickly and from the chest.

Unfortunately, chest breathing is quite common during normal functioning in our society. The shallowness of chest breathing reduces our oxygen intake and fatigues the body-mind. This effectively puts our body and mind in a state of constant anxiety and stress.

On the other hand, when we are calm and centered, such as we are when meditating, our breathing is significantly different. During these times, the breath fills us from the diaphragm through to our shoulders. We breathe slowly and deeply. It is no surprise that when we want someone to calm down, we inevitably tell him to "take a deep breath" and relax.

The control of the breath is an integral part of most spiritual, shamanic, and magical training. Through the breath, we can regulate our systems to allow ourselves to slip easily into trance. *Pranayama*, put very simply, is the yogic practice of breath control.

Prana, meaning the flow of energy of the Universe, is the link between body and mind. This flow of energy is vital to health and life. *Prana* moves through the breath. As Swami Rama describes, the "science of *pranayama* is thus intimately connected with the autonomic nervous system and brings its functioning under conscious control through the functioning of the lungs." [i]

This is the one exception to that rule we were all taught in high school biology: that the autonomic nervous system processes are involuntary. This is also where a student of any pagan path derives the greatest benefits. And this is one of the simplest and most powerful tools a parent can offer a child.

By consciously controlling our breathing, we can regulate our responses both to everyday reality and to our psychic experiences. Rather than instantly being thrown into a "fight-or-flight" fear response, which can paralyze the mind and spirit, we all have the ability to step back from the situation. Through the simple control of the breath, we can remain calm and centered, then view things from a much more confident and expanded perspective. This is also what enables us to enter trance states at will and with full control.

While it sounds simple, this may take some practice. The breath does not stop when we forget about it. It automatically kicks in and continues its habitual breathing pattern. Life has a way of taking our focus away from the breath. This is usually when the shallower chest breathing returns along with its associated tension and stress.

Children benefit greatly from learning to work consciously with the breath. Awareness and control can assist them in the release of attachments and fears, as well as in centering and opening to spirit guides. This can prevent unnecessary outbursts and arguments. It also has the potential to increase their control over their own behavior and help them to see situations with much wiser perception. You might consider guiding your children to be more aware of how they are breathing in everyday life, how it makes them feel, and how to change their breathing at will.

When I was in elementary school band, our teacher showed us a wonderfully simple way to determine just whether we were breathing from the chest or the diaphragm. Lying on your back, place one hand (or a light book) over the center of your chest and one on your abdomen. As you inhale, whichever hand rises indicates where your breath is entering your body. Deeper and slower inhalations bring more oxygen, more energy, and less stress. This type of breathing, called diaphragmatic breathing, invigorates the body.

Once you have developed an awareness of this, you can move on to slowing the breath. According to *Science of Breath*, it is considered average to breathe between sixteen and twenty breaths per minute. While *pranayama* is an involved discipline that also takes years to master, I offer you two exercises to practice with children. Both of these are very simple and will encourage the experience of calm and balance. These are particularly recommended for anyone who is experiencing pain, fear, or any type of emotional distress.

Breathing Exercise #1

Place your full attention on your breathing. Do not attempt to alter it; just observe for a few moments.

Where does your breathing seem to come from? How do you feel at this moment? If there is any tension in your body, where is it localized?

Now slow your breathing. Count to three on each inhalation and again, on each exhalation. Breathe deeply, filling your lungs from the bottom first. Feel your diaphragm stretch and expand as your abdomen moves out. As you exhale, feel your abdomen contract as the breath leaves from the bottom of your lungs first.

Breathe into any areas of tension or stress. Feel your breath fill and relax these areas. With each breath, tension and pain melt away.

Once you feel comfortable with this exercise, increase the count for inhalations and exhalations. Practice this several times a day, particularly when you are feeling stressed or are in pain.

Breathing Exercise #2

Recommended only for older children or for those who have easily mastered Breathing Exercise #1.

Beginning with Breathing Exercise #1, start to change the count of your inhalations and exhalations. Starting slowly, work toward a 1:2 ratio between inhalations and exhalations. For example, if your inhalation lasts for four counts, your exhalation will last for eight counts.

Do not increase this ratio too quickly. If you are gasping for air and desperately sucking in the inhalation, you should return to Breathing Exercise #1.

Dreaming

Kids are usually way ahead of adults in dreaming. They haven't yet assimilated those blocks and limiting beliefs that most adults have. As a result, they remember vivid and clear dreams. Many children will remember several dreams from the previous night. How many adults can say that?

The art of dreaming and dream interpretation was of particular importance to most ancient cultures. Dreams captivate us with possibility and wonder. In dreams, it seems, all things are possible. Dreams are not only bridges to our inner selves and our subconscious issues, they are frequently out-of-body journeys. Teaching children to use and control these abilities gives them the tools to self-knowledge and power. An individual who is able to master the dual nature of dreaming can do and create just about anything.

People who work intensively with dreaming learn to create and alter realities. They develop the ability to attune themselves completely to spirit guidance. They gain an experiential understanding that life is not what it appears in this reality through their conscious and deliberate journeying between worlds. What better gift to offer a child?

Dreams are a fun way to play with abilities without any pressure. It is part pretend, part exploration and investigation. Kids who are still masters at imaginative play are sure to be dream masters, too. Learning your own symbols is like cracking a code. It can easily be made into a game with plenty of storytelling involved.

Dream Interpretation

To teach dream interpretation, encourage your children to keep their own dream journal. If they cannot read and write well enough to do their own, you may want to keep one for them at first.

Begin by simply writing down everything that happened. The goal is to get into as much detail as possible. Asking questions as the child relates the story will help them access details they may have missed.

Try to cover the following aspects of each dream: Who or what was in it? What time of day or night did it take place? Where did it take place? What happened? When and where did each event take place? What was said or heard? How did the child feel at each point? See if you can get very specific about clothing, colors, sounds, smells, feelings, and the size and placement of people and things in the dream.

Once your child (or you) can access the details, move on to taking each piece of the dream as a symbol. For example, say the dream contained a big blue bus driven by a mouse. What is the first thing that comes to mind when you think of blue, a bus, big, a mouse, driving, etc? What types of things do you associate with each element? Then, do the same exercise for the whole picture, and the whole dream. We want to see the dream holistically as well as broken down into individual parts.

Encourage your children to share by setting aside a time to hear everyone's stories. Make it fun and be honestly interested in hearing what they have to say. Reciprocate and teach by example, through sharing your dreams as well. Allow your children's interest to stimulate your own openness and creativity and to help you regain control over your own dreaming. As we all know, parenting is a two-way street, a give-and-take relationship, in which we learn and grow at least as much as our children do.

Sometimes, a dream will appear to be so real that it couldn't be "just a dream." Occasionally, you will be aware that you are dreaming during the dream. These dreams are probably astral travels, or out-of-body journeys. This is also what is referred to as lucid dreaming.

The astral body is also known as *free soul* or *light body*. It is part of one's total energy: an energy body that is free to travel without the physical body. People have many differing beliefs regarding this. Some see it as a separate energy body that actually leaves the physical body and journeys to other realities.

Some people believe this is not truly another body and that we don't "go" anywhere, but our perception is sufficiently altered that we have access to other realities. There is no time or space, except in our own mental constructs in our three-dimensional experience. How you choose to view it is irrelevant as long as it works for you.

Children will almost always see this as a body double that is free to travel around without the physical body. When explaining this to children, be sure to let them know that the astral body is connected to the physical body by a silver cord. This means that the child cannot get lost outside the body. They can always find their way home by following that silver cord. I have included a Silver Cord Game in chapter 4.

Children learn by how we describe things and how we react. If we teach them that they can always get home by following that silver cord, they will believe that. We can be very convincing when our actions show that we believe it as well. In this way, the protection of the silver cord will become real for them. They will be comfortable traveling out of body and they will never get lost.

This is more than indoctrinating a beneficial belief. It is providing a tool to create realities and to manifest what is needed. We are giving them a head start on magic. After all, what is magic but the ability to effect change on one's reality?

It is not uncommon for parents and children to share dreams and to journey out of body together. My son and I have shared dreaming since he was born, though it happens less frequently the older he gets. I clearly remember playing and traveling with my mother when I was a child, while our physical bodies slept.

There is one night from my childhood that I remember vividly. I had been up and about at night as usual, without my physical body. I went to the foot of the couch where my mother was reading. I called to her. She whipped her head around to stare at me with wide eyes and got up to check on me (my body). I remember following her into the doorway of my bedroom. The sight of my physical body, in bed without me, was very unsettling. I was so startled that I was pulled immediately back into my body.

Parents should keep this in mind when responding to perceived calls in the night from their children. Your children may be wandering around without their physical bodies. This is normal and is nothing to be concerned about. Sometimes, they will come to us looking for comfort or play or whatever they usually come to us for while they are awake. But when we respond by going to their rooms and find they are still sleeping soundly, it is a good idea to send them some extra love. Believe me, the first time anyone sees his or her physical body from the outside can be very unnerving.

When our son had just moved into his own room, his free soul would often come to me on those nights when he was not sharing the family bed. We would cuddle for a while before I took him back to bed, as I always do when he physically falls asleep in my arms. I gently placed him down with his body and kissed him goodnight. In this way, the nightly excursions were not something unusual to which I react with ignorance or fear. He received his love and comfort and went back to bed. Consistency and calmness are key.

To help children work with lucid dreaming, you need to support and encourage them unconditionally. Children need their parents to believe and become excited right along with them. And it certainly doesn't hurt to play the dreaming games with them.

Parents should also work to become the best guides we are capable of being. Start simple and direct your explanations to the level of each individual child. If children have nightmares, begin by having them practice calling in spirit guardians or a parent. Also, have them experiment with changing their dreams. Perhaps they can walk out a door into a happy place or make friends with the monster.

Lucid Dreaming Exercises

Encourage your children to play with their dreams. They can experiment with going to familiar places or visiting loved ones. If you want to, you may be able to verify their information the next day. Have them meet with spirit guides or change objects in their dreams. Encourage them to allow their imaginations to run wild. Give them the freedom to create what they will. This is a stepping stone to creation in our reality as well as being one of the keys to self-knowledge.

Depending on the severity of a nightmare, you can play with changing these as well. You may want to begin by having your children practice being able to recognize they are dreaming and choose to wake up. With practice, children can develop great confidence in their abilities during dreaming and any trance work they may do in the future.

The easiest way to do this is to establish a dreaming cue. This is a sign that will alert children to the fact that they are dreaming. This often takes the fear out of a nightmare and allows children to regain control. People who practice looking at their hands in a dream often use this as a cue. They have inserted a hypnotic suggestion that, upon seeing their hands in a dream, they will realize they are dreaming and will be able to wake up whenever they choose. You might choose something fun or unusual for a child, perhaps the sight of a yellow balloon or a purple stop sign.

Dreaming Cue Exercise

To create an image as a dreaming cue, all you need to do is guide your child through a simple meditation.

Count down from ten to one. It may help to visualize going down a step for each descending number. Remind the child to periodically pause and take a deep breath into relaxation.

46

Imagine you are at your favorite place of relaxation. This can be a place you know of in this world or an imaginary place you visit in your mind.

Imagine that you are falling asleep. Feel yourself going deeper into relaxation.

(If your child does actually fall asleep, continue with the meditation. The child's consciousness is still able to follow your voice. You may choose to repeat this at another time when he or she is more able to stay awake throughout.)

You are now dreaming. Where are you? What is the temperature like? Is it day or night? Listen to the sound of your footsteps. Smell the air.

Now have the child visualize the cue you have decided upon. Involve as many senses as you can in really creating this cue. Spend some time making the visualization and experience of this cue as real and clear as possible. Say to your child that whenever he or she sees this image (be specific) he or she will instantly recognize that this is a dream. Repeat this twice. Continue by saying that whenever this image is seen, your child will be in total control of the dream. Repeat this twice. Say together that your child can awaken at any time and he or she can change or end the dream in any way.

You can always return to this place whenever you need to, and you will be safe and comfortable here.

Count up from one to ten. Stop periodically to remind your child that he or she is coming up slowly and that at the count of ten will be wide awake and feeling great.

Shared Dreaming

A great exercise for parents and children is shared dreaming.

Decide to meet each other one night. Discuss how you will set up your dreaming and what you will tell yourselves before falling asleep. See the section on Problem-solving Through Dreams for a simple way to set up dreaming. You may wish to begin by deciding on a familiar place to meet.

The next day, share your experiences. See how many details you can remember and how many images you share, even if your initial images do not include each other. Don't be discouraged if your memories don't match up. Either you have not yet learned your personal symbols or you just didn't remember that particular dream experience. Practice will improve your memory and ability.

Another wonderful way to work with dreams is use them for problem solving or guidance. In my family, we have used dreaming to find lost objects, to gain guidance in making decisions, and just for fun. This can be done in one of two ways.

Answer Fairies

Count down from ten to one, just before going to sleep.

Call on the Answer Fairies to come join you and help you answer your question.

What do the fairies look like? How many have come to play with tonight?

Greet them and thank them for coming to help you. Tell them what you want their help with. Be as specific as possible. (You may wish to discuss this in advance.)

Ask them to give you an answer by the next evening (or within three days).

Thank them for their help and for being your friends.

Allow your child to fall asleep as usual.

Problem-Solving Through Dreams

In order to set up dreaming, count down from ten to one just before going to sleep. In that calm, relaxed place, get a clear picture of the question or problem you are seeking to solve in your mind. Tell yourself that you will have a dream tonight that will give you the answer or some guidance to find the answer to resolution. State, with intent, that you will have the answer to your situation or that a path to this answer will be apparent by the following morning—and you will remember and understand it. Allow yourself to fall asleep. Although it may take some practice and a degree of trust, it really is as simple as that!

With all dreaming exercises, I recommend keeping a pad and paper right beside your bed. It is a good idea to write down (or use a tape recorder) everything you remember as soon as you wake up. Throughout the course of a day, or even just through the process of waking fully, many people will lose details of a dream. The entire dream itself may actually be forgotten as time passes.

There is one other possibility in dream recall. Some dreams may not be immediately accessible to the conscious mind upon awakening. For this reason, I suggest that older children and adults carry their pad and pencil with them throughout the day. It is quite common for a dream to be spontaneously remembered later in the day. It is also very possible that something you see or hear may spark the memory of the dream. I have had dreams brought to mind by billboards along the road, things people around me say, and even television commercials.

Telepathy

Telepathy is the ability to communicate on a non-verbal level. Some people may think of it as the ability to read minds. Telepathy is often distinguished from empathy as being more mental, while empathy is more emotional. Personally, I perceive the only real difference to be how the individual receives psychic information.

Some people pick up impressions from those around them in a "mind-reading" kind of way. They may receive words or pictures. Someone who tends more toward feeling is more likely to be empathic (not empathetic) and receive these impressions as emotions or sensory feelings. The telepath may know what someone is thinking; the empath feels their emotions and may even experience similar physical sensations.

We are all interconnected by Spirit. Some modern physicists believe that reality is really a holographic matrix of frequencies. We create our own reality by focusing on specific frequencies, thereby making them "real." Some modern physicists have described subatomic structures as a web that interconnects all entities. Pagans describe this as the Web of Life, and we do not limit it to physical life.

Our thoughts and emotions are out there in the Web for anyone to pick up on. Some of us shield better than others do, but there are plenty of people who unknowingly pick up on these psychic impressions. There are also those who would probe an unsuspecting person for information or simply for entertainment.

Why do pagan parents care about developing telepathy or any of these "psychic" abilities in themselves and their children? Well, for innumerable reasons that will vary according to the individual. These are abilities that expand our own experiences of our spirit guides, the God, Goddess, and the Great Spirit. They also increase our effectiveness in divination and healing.

So what are the ethics involved in telepathy or empathy? Do these ethics differ from those we apply to psychic/magical healing? And how does this vary from reading a person's tone of voice or body language? These are complex questions that could probably take up a book on their own.

Suffice it to say that we must do what we feel is right for us. In cases like this, the Wiccan Rede ("An it harm none, do what ye will") is a good guideline no matter what tradition you follow. In truth, the idea behind the Rede has its roots in many cultures and religions. However, your use of this as a guide will depend on your definition of harm and whether an invasion of privacy is applicable. Generally, we can go by spirit guidance or intuitive/gut feelings. If you question it or wouldn't be comfortable telling others about it, don't do it.

Some people make a distinction between reading what is out there for all to see and probing for deeper, more private information. In general, I tend to agree with this distinction. I believe that it is unethical and "harmful" to expect people to shut off their innate telepathic or empathic impressions for fear that they may learn something beneath the surface. If we were to go to this extreme, we may as well refuse to acknowledge any body language or tones of voice in communication. We may as well rely solely on email, where there are only the words given in a message to go on.

This is a tricky area for parents, especially psychic parents. In chapter 3, I described how we are connected to our children from pregnancy by one or more energy cords. It is through these cords that we intuitively know when our children are upset or injured. We often receive telepathic or empathic impressions through these connections.

Some parents will know exactly what a child is thinking, as though the child spoke the words. I will often ask my mother and my son to let me at least verbalize on occasion before they answer me. Similarly, I had to consciously stop answering our son's telepathic communications and make him speak to me when he was learning to talk. It had become far too easy to communicate on a purely psychic level and he was not verbalizing enough when I was around. Of course, now we can't get him to stop talking!

As I said, we receive these impressions in different ways. Most of us tend toward one or two areas, with less emphasis on the third. Many parents feel their children's wounds, whether physical or emotional, as though they were their own injuries. Others see visions of their children or hear a child cry or call the parent's name.

Most people who live together will develop a basic telepathic link. This is when we finish each other's sentences and just know what the other person is thinking and feeling without needing to say a word. Living together, especially as a family, harmonizes our energies and strengthens those energetic cords. So, working with your own children in this area is merely developing and honing interactions that are probably already occurring without your conscious recognition. This usually makes things very easy.

Telepathy can be a fantastic game to play with families. By the time I was a teenager, my mother and I had gotten so good at reading each other, we would joke about maybe using the telephone once in a while. The following are some of my favorite games from childhood, plus some new ones we have devised. They are listed in order of increasing age level.

Find Your Photo   ages 3 and up

This is a silly game that reminds many people of the testing games played by psychic experts on television shows. It can be played for prizes or simply for fun.

As the parent, it is up to you to decide whether receiving a prize for giving correct answers would create an issue for your child. If there is any doubt, it is probably best just to play for fun. For some children, there is likely to be enough competition, even in the absence of other players, without adding the additional element of a prize.

Start out by assembling some photos in manila envelopes. Include some of places your child has never seen (in this lifetime), one current one of the child or children, and a few of people, places, or animals that the child knows well. You can proceed in one of two ways. You can play double-blind, so that neither of you knows which photo is in which envelope, thereby eliminating the possibility that the child is picking up the image from your mind.

Or you can number the envelopes, keeping a list of what photo is in which number envelope. Then when you ask the child what the picture is, you can immediately gauge their accuracy and possibly coach them along. This is a good way to develop telepathy between the two of you and to establish a common set of symbols. This will also aid you in dream interpretation. Furthermore, it is an excellent tool for developing the clarity you may need if you ever receive disturbing impressions about your children.

Story Time   ages 5 and up

Now this can be a really fun and creative game!

Begin by making up a basic outline for a story. You may wish to write it all down as you play. Have one person be the StoryWeaver and start the story by telling a few sentences to get things moving. The StoryWeaver will then step back from the game and begin to send one image at a time to the group. This is the person who will direct the storytelling through projecting images and by jumping in verbally to get things moving again, if necessary.

Encourage the other players to say whatever pops into their minds spontaneously and weave that into the story. Allow yourself, as Story-Weaver, to pick up impressions from the other players and incorporate these as well. It may be necessary to create rules for the game, like taking turns.

The Newspaper Game   ages 7 and up

Using an unread newspaper, have each person select a page. Work with partners or in a group. Have the "sender" focus on a specific article at a time from their page. The "receiver(s)" communicate anything that comes to mind. Feel comfortable enough to communicate whether the sender needs to focus more or if the receiver(s) are "hot or cold." This is another fun way to work on accuracy and personal symbolism.

The Doctor Is In   ages 9 and up
This "game" is similar to the Newspaper Game in the partnering and receipt of psychic impressions.

Each person will come to the game with one or more "patient cases." These cases are either people who the guiding individual knows but the doctor-partner does not, or people from the news or other media who are in need of some type of healing. This does not need to be limited to physical healing.

The guiding partner will count the doctor down from ten to one and then give the doctor only the patient's name. As the doctor receives impressions, the guide continually meditates on the case at hand. The guide either confirms the doctor's findings or states that this information is unknown.

We rarely have complete and total knowledge of any individual and we do not want to tell the doctor that he or she is wrong unless we are absolutely certain of our facts. Information has come out of these sessions that was previously unknown, even by an individual's physician.

The doctor is encouraged to go with any impressions he or she receives, even if they do not initially appear to be related to the patient. As these impressions come through, the doctor may perform any healing he or she feels is necessary, from visualizing the patient healed to sending specific energy. The guide is also responsible for maintaining a grounding energy for herself and the doctor.

When the session is complete, the guide will either count the doctor back up for a debrief or continue with another patient. This is a choice to be determined by the parents and should be based on your child's ability to ground energy, maintain personal shielding, and his or her level of endurance. This game should never tire anyone out or leave someone feeling irritable or ill.

The debrief is a perfect way to end this type of game. It allows the situation to be discussed and the number of hits and misses to be evaluated. Sometimes, what may initially be regarded as a miss will be recognized as a hit when viewed from another perspective.

A perfect example of this is a story from my own experience with this game. I was approximately thirteen years old and playing this game with a friend of the family. When we got to my second patient, I could not get a clear image of anyone but a friend from school. I could not get

her out of my head. Now, sometimes, this is because another person requires our attention at that time.

However, in this case, it was a question of symbolism.
I said to my friend that I was getting nowhere and could
not get past this friend with brown hair that had just gotten a new hairstyle. I said I must need a break. My friend
was astounded because the patient also had brown hair and
had just gotten a haircut the previous day, completely
changing her hairstyle.

Psychometry

Psychometry games should always be played with
trusted individuals, especially when playing with children.

> Pass around personal items until no one is sure
> whose item they are holding. Have each person
> share what he or she is receiving from the item.
> Communicate any feelings, thoughts, mental pic-
> tures, etc. that the item triggers. This is an excel-
> lent way to hone accuracy and develop personal
> symbolism.

Working with the Aura

The aura, as most of us are aware, is the human energy
field. All living things produce an electromagnetic energy
field that can be measured or felt in various ways. I highly
recommend the works of Barbara Brennan and Rosalyn
Bruyere for anyone interested in working with the aura or
energetic healing.

The aura is made up of several levels, each corresponding to a chakra and an energy body. The following descriptions are my own perceptions of these levels. You and your
children may see them differently. Your perceptions may
differ slightly. Please keep in mind that each of these levels, while different, is interconnected with all other levels,
including the physical.

Within a few inches of the physical body is a web of white or blue-white energy. This seems to be easiest to see around the head.

Over that is a kind of cloud or energy mass, often initially seen as colorless. This is the emotional level, and with practice, one can perceive varying colors that can change according to one's emotional state. It is at this level that we first observe individual colors associated with chakras.

Next is another web, this time a white-yellow energy web. Changes in thoughts will alter this largely-mental level. These first three are generally believed to be those levels most involved in the creation and maintenance of the physical body.

The heart level is the point of balance, the first level above the physical. This is the level of the astral body. It appears to be very similar to the emotional body, but the colors are often more vibrant or intense.

Above this are the three spiritual bodies. The fifth level is generally seen in varying shades of blue and white, usually much deeper than the first level and vastly larger. This body is not limited to the physical form and expands into one of the first egg-shaped bodies.

The sixth level is often called the celestial body and is related to the "third-eye." This is like a star of colored light.

And finally, beyond that is the ketheric level. Kether is the Kabbalic crown, and this level is associated with the crown chakra. This is the golden luminous egg described by shamans and psychics and is quite likely the basis of the heavenly halo shown in paintings of Jesus Christ and the Christian saints.

I give this basic description as a guide. I also offer these words of advice: to see the individual levels takes a great deal of practice for most people, so don't feel bad if you can't see them at first. It may take a lifetime for most people to be able to separate these levels and to see all of them. However, there are many people who easily perceive the first few levels at different times, depending on a number of factors. This guide should help those people to understand what they are seeing.

Shake Hands

This is one of the simplest and most profound ways to learn to feel the human energy field.

It may help to rub your hands together before and after. If you wish, you may count down from ten to one beforehand, but this is usually not necessary.

> Sit or stand together. Hold out your hands as though you were going to shake hands. Stop just before actually touching the other person's hand. Notice any feeling or impression you get when your hands are very close together. Many people will feel a warmth, tingling, or resistance similar to touching two North (or two South) poles of a magnet together.
>
> Now play with this by slowly moving your hands further apart and then closer together. Be aware of any feelings or impressions that either person receives. Learn to trust your instincts. Practice this at different times to get a feel for how the aura changes. It will normally feel different after work or school than it might be after meditation or ritual.

Movie Star

Playing movie star is a great way to learn to see the aura. It is loads of fun and can often result in major giggle fits.

> Take turns standing before a plain, solid-colored wall or movie screen. The "audience" should center their energy and relax as much as possible. In the beginning, it is a good idea to

count down from ten to one or play this game after meditation.

Pay attention to the edges of the body of the movie star, particularly the head. Try not to fix your eyes on any one spot, but see if you can blur your vision or simply gaze at the star. As the star moves, you may notice an image that remains or follows behind his or her motions. Some people find this easier to recognize in the beginning as a true afterimage. They will watch, then close their eyes and see an image or colors in the basic shape of the person.

Movie stars that are into acting can call up different emotions, or play various parts for the audience. You might want to try this before and after a meditation or ritual. Watch to see the changes in size, shape, and color of the aura. If you do not see color at first or even for a long time, do not be concerned. Many people do not, and it is not important. There are other ways to gauge the condition of energy and the aura without the sight of color.

This is an exercise or game that is wonderful to play any time you are listening to a speaker. Speakers and lecturers tend to project a great deal as they speak, especially around the head. Again, do not stare or fix your eyes at any one spot, but watch and be aware of any images, particularly those around the edges of your visual field.

The Plant Experiment

The basic idea of this experiment is that plants respond to changes in the universal energy field. We can directly affect this field by directing our personal energy with a specific intent. So it is really plant magic.

In a distant approximation of scientific method, we will use a test subject and a control subject. Choose two plants of the same species, preferably the same age and condition. Do not change anything in your behavior or the environment of the control plant. The test plant will also remain in the same environment and receive the same food and water as the control plant. The only change will be directed energy to the test plant.

As pagans, we would never intentionally harm a living being, so we direct healing and loving energy to the test plant. Do this on a regular basis for a period of at least six months. Keep track of any changes in either plant. You will most likely notice an increase in growth or a deepened color in the test plant. There are certainly other variables that may interfere, especially when this experiment is performed in a home rather than in a completely controlled laboratory environment, but some type of change should be noticeable after six months.

There are a great number of games to play in this chapter, all having to do with some type of psychic ability. I offer these as suggestions for you to have fun and develop as a family. Don't attempt to do all of them at once. If this becomes at all stressful or ceases to be fun, put it on hold and go take a walk or play a mainstream game.

As pagans, we seek balance in all things. Psychic work must be balanced with ritual and physical work or play. A full day of meditation may be wonderful. But it is even more special and valuable if balanced with a bike ride or a game of baseball in the park. Our soul growth is not served by neglecting one aspect of Self in the hope of developing another. And our children need to be allowed to be children. To be honest, we adults need to be allowed to be children, too.

i.   Rama, Ballentine, and Hymes. *Science of Breath*, pp. 95.

Chapter 4
Protection and Grounding

Protection and grounding are two integral components of a fairly simple system that teaches children (and adults) to protect themselves and maintain a healthy balance in their own energy fields. Pagan parents are aware that non-physical energies affect their children, whether these energies come from other people, their own personal challenges, or from the Other Worlds.

To guide and protect their children effectively, parents must educate ourselves. Not only should they learn various protection methods, but they also must develop an understanding of these additional influences. This includes recognizing real threats from imagined ones.

Parents lead by example. When it comes to protection and guidance, particularly in the magical and psychic realms, they can do more harm than good if they allow their own imaginations and subconscious fears to run wild. It is essential that parents continue to work through their own stuff before they needlessly frighten their children.

Real vs. Imagined Threats

I have known pagan parents to freak out and terrify their children in situations that did not warrant those reactions. Sometimes this occurs after too many hours sharing scary stories with friends. But most often, it happens when families are present during unfamiliar rituals. Individuals who are completely new to the energies and experiences of some Deities and religions can easily over-react. I have seen parents misinterpret the effects of certain rituals to the point that they were asked to leave.

I remember one African ritual in particular. Several friends of the family were invited to observe an open ritual. One young man's parents were so wrapped up their fear of the unknown and the associated beliefs that this ritual had evoked some destructive energies that they were utterly unaware that they had terrified their son. He ended up sleeping with my family that night for protection. That truth was that these parents were simply unaccustomed to the feel of this particular pantheon and still held onto stereotypes about the religion involved. What occurred was normal for the ritual.

Many people love to be scared. The adrenalin rush from risky sports and horror movies can be addicting. Most kids love ghost stories, and quite often, so do their parents. The more realistic, the better. Plenty of pagans get together to share wild stories and personal experiences, especially when these people are relatively new to magic.

This is fine and it can be great fun. However, when we allow this to carry over into our behavior with our children, it has the potential to be damaging. Our children look to us to be brave and strong. They need to believe that we understand the world and the things we expose them to. They expect us to act accordingly.

When parents behave like children who have heard too many ghost stories and over-react, whether out of real fear or for the attention of others, their children experience these situations as real and frightening. They learn about the world through our behavior. We do them a disservice if we do not keep this in mind whenever we are with them.

The non-physical world can become something to be feared and mistrusted for children whose parents react in this way. If it is enough to freak out their parents, then surely it is truly frightening. Suddenly, the child finds something to fear everywhere. The physical world is frightening enough, but now the non-physical world holds the potential to become a horror movie. These fears will continue to affect the experience of these children.

When we permit our imagination and fear to get the better of us, we are limited, and potentially paralyzed, in our abilities to protect our families. Fear can create tremendous blocks. In many cases, it seems to short-circuit the brain, preventing us from using the abilities we have. Fear clouds the ability to see things as they really are, rather than how they appear through the filter of our fears and beliefs.

So how do you learn to separate perceived threats from the real thing? Well, experience is the best way. The more familiar you become with other paths and Other Worlds, the more you will understand the wide variety of spirits, traditions, and experiences that exist. This familiarity will allow you to determine what is a real threat and what is not.

Exploring and clearing your shadows is another excellent way to eliminate unnecessary fears and "see" with greater accuracy. This will also provide the clarity to recognize the threats from within (the projections of our own shadows) from those originating somewhere outside of us. As a result, you will develop a measure of strength and confidence that will diminish the number of perceived threats and increase your abilities to react appropriately in all realities.

In some circles, there is an over-emphasis on spells and outward-directed magic. I use the term "over-emphasis" because some individuals do not balance this with inner, personal work. I definitely understand the reasons why people avoid facing their innermost selves and accepting responsibility for their lives and experiences. It's a tough road and it can be a long process...but the benefits of doing this work are unsurpassed.

Wisdom and power flow through us. The ability to create reality and to perform effective spells also flows through us. Think of the body like a garden hose. The hose itself includes the physical and energy bodies, especially those associated with the physical realm. Unresolved issues create energy leaks and blocks. As power flows through us, it is lost through these leaks and is restricted by our blocks. Blocks can often create more damage than leaks as the building energy needs to find an outlet. The more issues we carry around, the less power we have available for creation.

This is the main reason for doing Shadow work. As you face and clear these issues, you become more complete, with significantly more energy to work with. You are stronger after having faced your own shadows. As a result, you frequently find less to fear outside yourself. Far less of your own stuff is being projected onto the worlds around you and suddenly you find yourself in a new, more comfortable reality.

Psychic Attack

Psychic attack most often takes the form of unconscious destructive energies that may or may not be directed at us. Although many people believe they are consciously attacked, this is rarely the result of a directed magical attack. It is far more commonly directed through anger as well as both conscious and repressed hostility or jealousy.

When we allow holes to remain in our personal energy fields, we leave the doors open for any passing energies to enter our fields. Whether conscious or unconscious, the thoughts and feelings of other people, even if they are not related to us, can affect us if we remain unaware of these factors. Children, especially very young children, are particularly susceptible to this because of their relative lack of chakra filters.

Psychic vampires engage in a subtle and often unconscious form of psychic attack. They are people who need everyone else's energy constantly. We may feel tired or depleted around them. Often, they will create minor crises in order to get the group energy level higher. They tend to be what my husband and I call the long-huggers. They seem to hang on for dear life and for an eternity, sucking your energy as they hug you.

Most of the time, psychic vampires are adults. Unfortunately, since they are often unaware of what they are doing, they will drain anyone, including children. Children are vibrant and full of life. They exude the energy flowing through them effortlessly. Like strong adults, children often attract people who are no longer able to feel that life force flowing through them.

Some of these vampires may even be parents who have become so beaten down by life or so hurt that they effectively switch places with their children. They depend on their children for their own emotional well-being. Frequently, they will live vicariously through their children, having no real life of their own. They unconsciously maintain an emotional (usually guilt-driven) hold on their children that can prevent their children from fully living their own lives as adults.

Before I get into specific methods of protection, I would like to discuss the effects of resistance during any form of psychic attack. Many pagans believe that they must always offer some type of barrier or perform some sort of spell to protect their families. This is not necessarily the case. Resistance itself provides additional and undesirable energy that can intensify and prolong the situation.

The effects of resistance can be likened to an encounter with an annoying or pushy individual. When confronted by someone like this, sometimes the best course of action is not to get defensive or upset. Many times, the best way to handle these people is simply to let it go and walk away. The offending individual is then immersed in his own drama. He has no response from us to latch onto and use. Energetically, this is frequently the case as well.

Often, the best thing we can do is recognize that unwanted energy is there and simply allow it to pass by us. Resistance and fear create obstructions that hold this energy within our own auric fields. Our emotional reactions to this energy, and our often incorrect assumptions about its intent and source, appear to be almost sticky, like glue or gum. This not only holds onto any energies directed at us, but it attracts and binds to any passing thought forms that may be similar to the energy we are resisting.

Teaching children to trust in the God and Goddess or Great Spirit and in their helping spirits can reduce the possibility that they will automatically create this type of block or "glue." This is the first and best defense against psychic attack. Children who are able to release honestly any attachment, any resistance, to incoming energies will not provide the opportunity for these energies and thoughtforms to stay with them. Lacking energy to feed off, they will simply pass by that child in search of another source of emotion.

I should say that it can be difficult to reach the point where you honestly offer no resistance or judgments. Unless you truly offer nothing for these beings to feed off of, other measures are probably your best bet.

Sacred Space

Creating a safe, sacred space is the first step in protection and security. Maintaining a healthy energy in your home is an important part of that. But sometimes, you need a little help. It is during these times that purification and protection rituals are needed.

In our family, we follow up particularly difficult days by smudging and drumming. We smudge each other and either the room or the entire house, depending on why we feel the need for clearing. We may call in spirit guardians,

Deities, and the energies of the directions, asking for their guidance and protection. Not only does this invoke protective and purifying energies, but it also creates a mindset for our son that he is safe and secure.

At the age of three, our son had his own feathers to move the smoke around while I held the burning herbs. By three and a half, he was allowed to hold a wrapped smudge stick. By four years old, he had created his own smudge fan and began to join me on sagebrush picking expeditions, which will be discussed in a later chapter. Now he is allowed to light smudge or burn incense in his room, with permission. In these ways and others, he is learning to bolster the energy of security and to create his own sacred space.

We have created our home and yard as a sacred space by regularly honoring the spirits and each other. In doing this, we give back something of what we receive throughout our lives as we continue the cycle of energy. This channels protective energy through our home. It makes for a very calm and centered atmosphere.

Shielding

Shielding is controlling how we leak or broadcast thoughts and emotions. To shield effectively means developing the ability to create boundaries and to plug up the leaks in your energy field.

Not only does this give you some privacy, but it also increases your personal power. When you continually leak energy, you allow holes to remain in your energy field. That garden hose I described earlier loses energy through these holes.

But more than that, other people can drain your energy much more easily when you are unaware of holes or blocks in your energy field.

Without a conscious awareness and ability to control your own energy field, you open yourself up to psychic vampires as well as to psychic attack. Children are particularly vulnerable to this.

Shielding is a wonderful way for kids and their parents to seal off their energies and maintain a healthy system. As soon as your kids are old enough to follow directions and perform a basic visualization, they are ready to learn to shield. Parents often need to learn to shield for young children until they get to the point where they can effectively manage their shields on their own.

Any child whose language and comprehension skills have not yet developed to the point where he or she can understand your descriptions of shields, let alone understand what the point of shields are, is obviously not ready to learn these techniques. Unless children are ready to handle it on their own, it is our responsibility as parents to do it for them. To be honest, I don't know too many parents who stop doing it, even when their kids can do it for themselves...that's just what parents do.

Earlier in this book, I explained how the energy field of a parent shields and filters outside energies when a child is in contact, such as sitting in a parent's lap. I also described how as children grow, they leave filaments of their own energy on "their" people and things. This is the basis for the first exercise in shielding your children.

Shielding for Children

Visualize your own energy flowing to your children and merging with their energy. As it flows through the cord that connects you, it becomes a bubble of white light surrounding them completely.

As you send this energy, hold the intent that this semi-permeable boundary creates a sacred space around each child. Say to yourself that this protective bubble prevents any and all unwanted beings, energies, and influences to reach your child, while it allows all the universal love and goodness to freely flow through. Also remind yourself that your own filters will not permit any of your stress or negative energies to pass through to your children.

Call upon whatever Deities or guides you work with and ask for their guidance and assistance in shielding and protecting your children.

Check to be sure that the bubbles completely surround them with no holes. You should periodically check for any tears or leaks, especially if there has been any stress or unhappiness around either you or your children.

The Egg of Protection

This is an exercise that can be learned as soon as a child knows what an egg is, can understand simple directions and has begun to engage in imaginative play. It should be a great game of make-believe in order to keep it fun and creative for the child.

Have your children take a really good look at an egg. You may want to have very young children inspect a plastic or hard-boiled egg, unless you feel like cleaning up a mess. Let them really inspect it from all sides.

Now tell them that you are going to play a game. Tell them to close their eyes and imagine an egg surrounding them. Ask them what their eggs look like: what colors they are and what else they see inside their eggs.

Tell them that they are going to make beautiful white shells on the outside of their eggs. Really get them to use their imaginations and create shells that go all the way around each child on all sides. Let them know that they need to make sure there aren't any holes, so that the inside of the egg won't leak. Encourage them to see their shells as glowing or sparkling white.

Older children may want to add outward-facing mirrors, additional shells of fire, or anything else that spurs their imaginations and makes them feel safe.

While they are doing all this, use your own imaginative or telepathic abilities to watch what they create. If you see any holes, let them know. Tell them what great jobs they are doing and how beautiful their shells look. Ask them for permission before making any changes or fixing anything in their shells.

Ask them occasionally how their eggs are doing. Tell them how your egg is, so it becomes a game you play together. You may want to play the egg game again periodically, to check for holes and continue to develop their abilities in this area. Keep in mind that you can erect an Egg of Protection around infants, pets, a home, property, tent, office, or your car.

Spirits of Place

It is always a good idea to develop a loving and honoring relationship with the "Spirits of Your Place." Even when we go camping or backpacking, my family and I always honor the Spirits of Place first and ask their welcome and protection for as long as we will be there. We leave a suitable offering when we arrive and when we leave.

At home, you can make it a normal family practice to thank the Spirits of Place at each meal or each time you enter your home. You may want to create a special altar for the spirits who contribute to your protection and the harmony of the home. Or you may simply include some symbol for them on your family altar.

Amulets

We can also use amulets and talismans in protecting our home. Many pagans use bottle spells or bury amulets around the house for protection and the maintenance of good health, harmony and prosperity. Some people will bury one item in either a central location or around the perimeter at each of the directions, while others hang pouches and amulets inside the house.

Involving children in the creation of amulets, talismans, or altars for the house is an excellent project. It helps them to feel like an integral part of the family while it teaches them and empowers them. Simply by holding the belief that these methods will keep them safe, children will feel more confident and will attract safer situations.

Home Protection Amulet

Begin by creating a large disk of clay with your children. Write your names on it or simply write "Protection" and include a drawing of the house. You may choose to make up a simple chant for protection and write that on one side of the clay disk. Make it a simple, easy chant that your children will be able to recite with you when you charge the amulet. Something like this works well with young people:

> *Spirits of this Place, I pray,*
> *Bring us protection, harmony, and play.*
> *Guard us and our privacy.*
> *Let in only happy energy.*

Once the disk has been baked or air-dried, wrap it in a red or black cloth until you are ready to charge it with your family's energy and your chant.

71

Prepare your altar with black and/or white candles and either Dragon's Blood or essential oil of cedar, frankincense, rosemary, or sandalwood.

Count yourself and your children down into a light trance state. Thoroughly smudge, or purify in your usual manner, your entire home. Really clear it out and see it filled with white light.

Cast a Circle or call upon the Spirits of the directions in your usual manner. Call in any helping or guardian spirits that your family members work with and ask their assistance in this rite.

Count down from ten to one again into a slightly deeper trance state.

Bring out the clay disk and hold it in your hands. Have your family members hold hands around you. Each person on either side of you should place one hand on your arm nearest that person. Guide everyone present to direct his or her attention and focus to the disk as you recite your protection chant.

Go around the circle and allow everyone to state any specific needs they have that they would like the amulet to assist with. These should be general or specific family protection, happiness, or success issues, and they should be very important. As ritual leader, you should be funneling these prayers into the disk.

Repeating your special chant or prayers, allow everyone to anoint the disk with the Dragon's Blood or essential oil. Guide them to feel the disk filling with this energy. Then wrap the disk in the red or black cloth and close the ritual, thanking all spirits and Deities that were called for assistance.

You may choose to bury the disk immediately after the rite or later on. Just be sure that each person who participated in the rite is present for the burial. Once the disk is fully buried, have everyone place their hands on the ground over the disk. Guide them to feel the energy of their prayers radiating out from the disk and surrounding your home. Once again, give thanks to the Earth Mother and all helping spirits.

Spirit Guardians

Many children respond well to cartoon or animated hero characters. They believe these beings are real in a way, particularly younger children. They can relate to these characters. It also helps that these types of animated beings are not intimidating the way a large animal or Deity may be. Often, these images can be good role models or teaching guides on their own.

The guides and guardians of children often manifest in this way, using these characters as safe and familiar channels that children can more easily relate to. Storybook characters, stuffed animals, and television heroes all have the potential to bring blessings and protection to children. Cookie Monster loves to eat everything and may be a wonderful guardian for dreamtime. Thomas the Tank Engine carries us away from frightening things and into wonderful places. And older sci-fi fans can always erect a force field for protection. Talking animals and trees, singing wind and water, friendly dragons, and fairies are all age-appropriate images to learn of their interconnections with All of Life.

Parents are often the first ones to have insight into who some of their children's guides may be. You walk into their room one night, and there is this energy set up as if it belongs and your child is perfectly comfortable in its presence. That's a good clue that a spirit ally has taken an interest in your children.

My mother was aware of Bear by the time I was four or five years old. Bear was a permanent force at the foot of my bed for years. For our son, the first two spirit allies I was aware of were Thor and a dragon when he was just weeks old. I find it very interesting that suddenly Karl has dedicated himself to Thor—I probably only told him about that once years ago.

On the other hand, our children often have very private interactions with their spirits, and we may be surprised to discover the allies they have connected with. My mother never saw the spirit man, a *tomten* or *saivo* man, who walked me to and from the bus stop each day and who still turns up whenever I am being targeted by damaging influences. In addition to Thor, I never imagined the connections our son would have to Bald Eagle and Krishna, with whom I had a major connection at the same age.

The truth is that we may or may not have a conscious awareness of the spirits our children connect with. Either way, it is important that we support these connections, even if they are not anything we would have imagined. And no matter who they connect with, we do have the ability to honor and work with those beings, too, mainly when our children are young.

Connecting with Spirit Guides

Because of their limited language, infants, and young toddlers can't describe their guides to us. It is rare for a child this young to see a photo and say "That's It!" So parents frequently don't know who to call on for protection blessings for their children. Many parents will simply invoke the God and Goddess or Great Spirit. Other parents ask the blessings of their personal or clan spirit guardians, ancestors, or the Deities of their tradition.

This is done just as you normally would do it for yourself. Call upon these spirits in your usual manner. If you normally make offerings, do so. Then ask them to extend their blessings to your children, guiding and protecting them. You may also ask them to help you contact the child's personal spirit guardians. You may also use the Meeting Your Child's Spirit Guides exercise from chapter 1.

Even if you do not know who or what guides and guardians work with your children yet, you can still call upon these beings to help them. After doing the Egg of Protection or Shielding exercises, call upon "the spirit guardians of _____." Ask them for their guidance and assistance in shielding and protecting your child.

When connecting with the guides of your children, be open to whatever may happen. You may be surprised by who or what you encounter. Know that you have the right to ask any questions you need to be sure this is a beneficial guide—but know also that they don't have to answer you.

You may receive vital information in guiding your child through his life. On the other hand, depending on the state of your life or the child's environment, be prepared for some questions or demands from the guides you contact. They may even offer some guidance in how you may improve the situation for your child. A good rule of thumb when dealing with spirits is: if you are not ready for the answers, don't ask.

To guide older children, usually over the age of four, in developing a relationship with their guides, begin by invoking their guides with the children in the room. Let them observe and ask any questions. Ask them how they feel when the guides respond or show up. Encourage your children to help you call on their guides. They may want to call their guides silently in their own minds or start with some simple phrases said out loud.

Be aware of any animals your children have a special affinity for. Even a baby may show distinct preferences for certain animals. These may very well be animal allies, also known as totem or power animals. When these animals show up, create a simple altar for images of them.

An altar does not need to be the traditional flat surface for holding special items. For children, it can take the form of room decorations, stuffed animals, clothing, bedding, or amulets hung on the doorknob. The idea is to bring that energy, in a concrete form, into your children's presence. In doing so, you are strengthening the bond and making a type of offering, or perhaps more of an honoring, of these spirit guides and guardians.

Older children can be taught to call on these animals during dreams and anytime they feel uncomfortable or threatened. You might have your children visualize the animal coming to their aid and "getting" the scary monsters under the bed or giving them the strength to speak up in class. Let them know that invocations can be as subtle and silent as necessary so they can connect with guides anytime and anywhere.

Nighttime Protection

Most families have nighttime rituals. They may include bath-time, storytelling, and maybe a bedtime prayer. Pagan families can alter this traditional bedtime ritual to fit their own beliefs and needs. These rituals are important because children tend to feel more vulnerable at night.

They are often alone—in their own rooms, in the dark—when everyone else is sleeping. Their imaginations can run wild at times like this. If they are not prepared for spirit contact, they may be frightened by a visit from a departed loved one or the appearance of a fairy.

At that point between sleep and awake, we are all more open to other realities. Children may be unnerved by a conscious awareness of Other Worlds or the initial stages of astral travel. Whether their fears are grounded in imagination, too much television, life experiences, or other reality, we can help them feel more comfortable going to sleep.

One important thing parents can do is educate their children on the difference between the media and reality. Movies about monsters and terrifying ghosts sell well at the box office, but they are not real. Even if your kids don't watch these movies, it can be nearly impossible to shield them completely from these images. Children need to understand that these are not the images they are likely to see when they connect with spirits.

Developing some comfort with spirit beings and other realities as a pagan parent is always a good idea. Then you can more easily communicate that comfort to your children. Many of the exercises and games in this book are specifically designed to increase children's sense of safety and familiarity outside the physical body. The benefits need not be limited to children. Parents may gain just as much from sharing in these exercises.

To help children feel more secure while they are asleep, aware of other realities, or out of their bodies, you can start talking about these things when they are still quite young. Be proactive about this and find out what they think and what they believe early on. Let your children know that everyone travels about during dreaming and remind them that we are all familiar with this type of journeying. We did very well without our bodies before we chose these bodies to live in and we easily remember all we need to know once we are dreaming.

Discussions and working with the exercises in this book can make nighttime fun for most children. But there still may be nights when they just do not feel prepared to handle being alone, especially after a difficult day or a nightmare. They may need you to check their beds for bugs or look under beds and in closets for monsters. They may just need you to come when they call you in the middle of the night, simply for reassurance that if something ever really did happen, you would be there for them.

You might consider being willing to sleep with your children or allow them into your own bed for comfort and security on particularly intense nights. In fact, many parents allow their children to sleep in the "family bed" for years. This is particularly true in many native cultures around the world.

One of the first and best ways to empower your children at night and at any time is to tell them about the silver cord that connects them all to their bodies. Better yet, you can help them experience this and become confident in its ability to bring them safely home. The Silver Cord Game is a great way to do this.

Silver Cord Game

Go outside with your children on a nice day or find comfortable spots next to a window. Lie down and watch the sky. Pretend that you are rising up away from your bodies into the sky. Really get into it. Soar like birds, float with the clouds, pretend you are a kite, become One with the sunlight.

As you rise, remind everyone to look back and see the silver cord behind them, connecting them to their physical bodies on the ground. Suggest that this is exciting and fun. It is usually best not to mention negatives (like being frightened) unless someone brings it up. Describe the shining, strong silver cord and say that no matter where you go, you can always find your way back by following the cord. Tell them that it is unbreakable. It can be wound into knots and go as far as they can, but it will always bring them home.

Play with this for a while and then guide them to follow the cord back to their physical bodies. Tell them to feel their bodies, their breathing, the floor or ground beneath them. Then have them open their eyes and return to everyday awareness.

Nightmares

Nightmares are no fun for anyone. Children get scared, and everyone loses sleep because of them. A parent's first instinct is usually to awaken the child out of the nightmare immediately. This is usually fine. However, some pagan parents will assume the recurring nightmares are the result of some form of psychic attack.

In truth, this is rarely the case. It is far more likely that your children have past or present life issues to work through. They will continue to experience nightmares until the issues are cleared. It is not always in their best interests to prevent an uncomfortable situation or to avoid something troublesome or even painful. This is part of the human experience, and we all grow through these times—difficult though they may be.

However, there are things you can do to assist your children through the issues and the nightmares. You might try grounding out excess energy while your child sleeps (see below). You may want to work with shared dreaming to provide support and security during dreaming. It may help your children to talk about their dreams or to keep journals. It is best to follow your intuition or spirit guidance in these situations.

I want to suggest again that you not hesitate to use the family bed when necessary. We all need to be close to those we love when we are going through a difficult time. Children need this closeness even more than adults, due to their relative lack of chakra filters and control over their own energy fields. This is similar to a child seeking protection by sitting in a parent's lap, as discussed in earlier chapters. However, while we sleep, we tend to be more psychically open and vulnerable.

To a child, nighttime fears and experiences are just as real as any physical, daytime experience. In fact, they can be more frightening because of the lack of light and physical comfort. While not for everyone, parents need not fear they are encouraging weakness or allowing manipulation if they allow their children to share their beds when they need comfort or security.

One fun way to take the pressure out of bedtime is to devise your own nighttime prayers and lullabies. They are invocations for children and as such, should be kept simple. This process can encourage a feeling of protection and empowerment. Children love to rhyme and rhymes tend to be more easily remembered.

A Bedtime Prayer

> Now I lay me down to bed.
> Great Spirit, bless my sleepy head.
> As I journey through this night,
> My silver cord will hold me tight.
> Mother Earth and Father Sky,
> Watch over me here where I lie,
> For tomorrow I will greet the day
> With love and joy and lots of play.

Review the Day

We have found that a nightly review of the day is a great way to clear some of the more troubling things that may creep back as nightmares. It also helps children to focus on the positive elements of each day and guides them in finding creative ways to face their challenges. This process is better suited to older children who are developing language and critical thinking abilities.

Some families like to spend some time before bed talking about the day together. This strengthens family bonds and keeps the lines of communication open between you and your kids. It can be time consuming, but there are many children who really benefit from this time with a parent.

Some older children prefer to write in a journal by themselves. This gives them some privacy with their thoughts and allows them to vent about challenges with other family members that they don't feel ready to discuss openly yet. Some people also think things through more easily when they write.

However you do it, this is a simple review of the day's events. What draws your attention? What do you feel is unfinished? What do you wish you had done differently? Did you live that day to its fullest? Did you tell those you love how much they mean to you? If you choose to, you may make plans for the next day based on this review.

Grounding Energy

The ability to ground energy is just as important as shielding. When we ground energy, we send unnecessary or unwanted energies into the Earth for release and purification. There are five main energy centers that are responsible for grounding: the root chakra, the chakras in the soles of both feet, and the chakras in the palm of each hand.

As I discussed in the Incarnation chapter, our energy progresses down the physical body and grounds us, through the root chakra, into this body and this reality. While energy constantly flows in and out of all our energy centers, our root chakra is the main grounding cord. This can be seen as a cord of energy, extending deep into the Earth. This cord naturally funnels off excess and undesirable energies.

We are also naturally grounded through the soles of our feet. These are minor chakras. However, they are very important in feeling anchored and connected to the strength and support of the Earth. They also will funnel off excess energy, although to a lesser degree than the root chakra.

There is a chakra point in the palm of each hand as well as in the tips of each of our fingers. Although these are minor chakras, they are used continually. They can become very strong and sensitized, especially in the hands of healers. It is through these chakras that we send and receive sensory and emotional impressions of our world and other people. With regard to grounding energy, the palm chakras in particular are vital chakras to develop.

There are two basic reasons to ground energy. The first has already been touched upon here. People can, for a number of reasons, accumulate an excess of energy in their auric fields. This energy can overload your system, resulting in anything from a spacey feeling and lack of focus to fainting. This build-up of energy can also prevent you from receiving beneficial energies because the flow through you has been blocked.

The second main reason to ground energy is to prevent you from taking on other people's energies. When you pick up the energies of other people, without a way to let them go, you risk manifesting any associated mental, emotional, or physical ailments. People will get headaches or feel anger that does not belong to them.

While some people may find this clear indication that metaphysical beliefs are real, it is not cool or funny to allow it to continue. There is no reason to get other people's issues. We are of no benefit to anyone if we begin to exhibit their symptoms. And this does not teach children anything about holding their own power and staying healthy.

Grounding is generally so natural that even the youngest children (with some degree of language skills) can learn to do this. However, I believe there to be a correlation between one's astrological make-up and one's innate ability to ground energy. I would recommend that parents review their children's astrological charts with an expert to determine whether there is a need for additional practice in grounding. The exercises below are fun and effective for nearly everyone. Parents with infants can bring their children into these meditations and perform the exercises for them.

Shower Time

This is a great exercise that can be used either as a simple meditation or as a more active meditation in the shower or in the rain.

Count down as usual from ten to one.

Imagine a shower of clear, white light over your head. Feel this light-water on your face and your hair. Let it flow over your entire body.

Feel your tensions and worries dissolve in the water. As the water passes over your body, it washes away all unwanted or excess energies from your head down. See and feel the light fill you from your head down.

Look down at the drain and see these unwanted energies spiral away. These may look like different colored water or symbols or images of people or events. Trust whatever you see and let it go.

Continue to feel these energies drain from your body as you are filled with this light. If any place on your body seems tense or uncomfortable, direct the shower to that place until it is relaxed and clear.

Enjoy this feeling of light. See the light flow out of every pore of your body. It shines forth through your eyes and your hair and your hands and feet.

When you are ready, count back up from one to ten.

Hug The Earth

Children love this exercise almost as much as they love hugging trees, which can also help us ground energy. It is fun to lie down and try to hug the Earth, especially when a parent or sibling plays along.

Lie down on your stomach on the Earth. This may be on dirt or grass as long as there is no man-made interference between you and the ground.

Stretch your arms out and hug the Earth. Press your hands in as you try to hug the whole Earth.

Now feel any unwanted or excess energies gently seep out of your body into the Earth. As you hug Her, Mother Earth is taking away all these energies that you do not need. Feel them trickle out of your hands and the center of your body. Notice where you feel them drain from the most.

Continue to lie there and allow the Earth to pull out these energies. After a while, you will feel Earth energy flowing back up into your body. If you feel more comfortable, you may turn over and lie on your back at this point.

Allow the energy of the Earth to fill you with radiant light as the Earth returns your hug. Feel Her love for you and Her strength. Thank the Earth before you get up and go on with your day.

*After using this exercise for a while, you and your children will be attuned to the Earth energy and you will be aware of where on your bodies the energies seem to build up. At this point, you can alter this exercise so that you can send these energies into the Earth at any time and in any place without lying down.

Earth Star Balancing

This exercise is designed either alone or in conjunction with any type of grounding exercise. It restores energy flow while it balances the chakras. Some of the wording for the chakra section may need to be changed for younger children. For example, a child who does not know what the solar plexus is should be able to understand "the middle of your belly."

Count yourself down from ten to one as usual.

See a ball of light at the center of the Earth. See this light flow up out of the Earth's core and into your body through the soles of your feet and the base of your spine. Feel this energy fill your entire body. Feel it pour out from the pores of your skin, your eyes, your hair, your navel. Feel it flow completely though you and out through the top of your head. Fully experience this flow.

See a star at the center of the Universe. See its light flow down from the center of the star and into your body through the top of your head. Feel this energy fill your entire body. Feel it pour out from the pores of your skin, your eyes, your hair, your navel. Feel it flow completely though you and down into the Earth. Fully experience this flow.

Experience both of these flows together for as long as you like until you really feel them. See and feel your total energy space cleansed and purified by this light. Your body appears to be a long cord of white light.

Now see a ball of violet light coming from the top of your head. It is like a purple bead on your cord of light. Feel and see this beautiful violet energy. Stay with this ball of light until you fully experience it.

At the center of your forehead is deep, dark blue ball of light, another bead on your cord of light. Feel and see this beautiful deep, dark blue energy. Stay with this ball of light until you fully experience it.

In the middle of your throat is a ball of bright blue energy. Feel and see this beautiful bright blue energy. Stay with this ball of light until you fully experience it.

In the center of your chest, right by your heart, is a beautiful ball of green energy. Feel and see this beautiful green energy. Stay with this ball of light until you fully experience it.

Move your attention down to the ball of golden energy at your solar plexus. Feel and see this beautiful golden yellow energy. Stay with this ball of light until you fully experience it.

In the middle of your abdomen, see a ball of vibrant orange energy. Feel and see this beautiful orange energy. Stay with this ball of light until you fully experience it.

At the base of your spine is a deep red ball of energy. Feel and see this beautiful red energy. Stay with this ball of light until you fully experience it.

See these balls of energy on the cord of white light that is your body. Feel how it feels to be fully relaxed and balanced.

Above all, the best way to keep children safe and balanced is to teach them by example how to live an honorable, respectful life. When parents live their lives in this way, they are guided and protected by the spirits around us. In honoring this guidance and placing themselves in the flow of universal energy, the abundance of the universe flows to them. All of their needs are taken care of and live in a much freer and happier space, no matter what life sends their way.

Many people believe that we choose our lives and our deaths before we re-enter this world. While we can certainly alter these plans as we go along, we don't always remember why we chose what we did or even that we chose it. The process of incarnation, coupled with living in this reality, can have a tendency to block our memories of the time spent between lives.

There are certain events that we will experience, whether we chose them before incarnating or created them while we were here. We cannot protect our children from everything. And if we could, we would be depriving them of valuable growth opportunities. We can help them to handle these things in the best possible way by teaching them that every situation and every being we encounter is a potential teacher.

If we can teach our children how to use each experience and to grow from it and if we can live this way ourselves, we offer them the tools they need to create truly happy lives. This is a lesson that goes beyond this one lifetime. It is a tremendous contribution to the evolution of their souls. What better gift to those who have chosen us as their parents for this lifetime?

Chapter 5
Health and Healing

How many times have you heard the term *Doctor Mom* or *Doctor Dad*? We may or may not have gone to medical school, but we learn an amazing amount of stuff simply through being with our children as they grow up. Parents become lay experts in all kinds of healing techniques, from understanding that simply applying a Band-Aid will often fix a toddler's "owie" and knowing what to do for diaper rash to knowing what antibiotics are prescribed for what conditions and being able to identify correctly many of the bones and muscles of the human body. This is borne out of necessity. The fact is that kids get sick and kids get hurt. And the responsible parent learns as much as possible about each incident.

I should begin by stating that the healing sections of this chapter are not intended to function as training manuals. I do give an overview of alternative healing techniques as well as some very basic physiology. If you plan to use these or other methods, I would strongly encourage you to investigate further. Please see the Recommended Reading section at the back of this book for more information.

Healing is not something to be taken lightly. Training and education are vital to your success as a healer, even if you are only using these abilities within your own family. I recommend learning about anatomy and physiology as you research your favorite alternative healing methods.

The medicine cabinet takes on a whole new meaning in a pagan home. Most medicine cabinets are filled with over-the-counter drugs for colds, pain, insomnia, rashes, etc. In pagan homes, there are often several "medicine" cabinets ranging from the variety of herbal teas in the kitchen to the homeopathics and flower remedies in the bathroom. Pagan families keep an assortment of healing stones, massage oils, meditation mats, audiocassettes or CDs, and aromatherapy gadgets in rooms all over the house.

This use of alternative remedies carries over to the pagan first-aid kit. My mother jokes that, although I carry around a backpacker's first-aid pouch, she can't even get an Excedrin out of me. Although I do carry acetaminophen and ibuprofen, she has a point. My kit is filled with homeo-pathic and flower remedies, a snake-bite kit, an assortment of bandages and gauze, pads soaked in hydrogen peroxide and other assorted items.

I grew up using homeopathic remedies and herbs. When I was a child, homeopathics were called tissue or cell salts, and there were only about twelve of them available. Today health stores carry several brands providing both mixtures for different ailments and single remedies. Herbs are no longer limited to health-food stores. They can be found in many mainstream grocery stores and even in some bookstores.

With exceptions for certain conditions that require medical intervention, our son has only been treated with homeopathics, energy work, massage, diet, and other as-sorted natural methods. In addition, I research all condi-tions that he develops and all interventions that he re-quires, including vaccinations. I make certain that I have all the information I need to make informed choices about his treatment.

Except in extreme cases, this refusal to follow blindly the dictates of modern medicine is something the pagan community should be proud of. We think for ourselves, and we tend to be avid self-educators. When it comes to the well-being of our children, we will not simply bow to accepted practices, particularly if those practices are questionable. In this way, pagan parents offer their children even more valuable tools to create better lives for themselves.

Throughout this book, I have described the impact of the shadow side on our children's well-being and on our own psychic and magical abilities. This also plays a role in maintaining one's health. Although children generally have far less submerged in the shadow side than do adults, it can still create health issues for them. While these primarily show up as emotional or behavioral situations, imbalance can cause problems on any level of being. For children, keeping a daily journal, having consistent and honest discussions with parents, and doing various meditations are the best ways to encourage self-knowledge—and to discourage repression.

Healing Stones

There are scores of books available today on the various uses of stones and crystals. As a pagan, you may have come to your spiritual path through an interest in stones. Most pagans know at least a little about the meanings of some stones. We work with stones in a wide variety of ways. Many of us wear jewelry with specific stones that feel right to us or carry the vibrations we wish to bring into our lives. Some of us, especially children, will carry a stone or two in our pockets. In pagan homes, stones can be found just about everywhere.

For healing, it is a good idea to keep the stones on or near your body as much as possible, and to meditate with them. If you are working with a specific stone, you will need to keep it with you at all times for at least twenty-four hours; some people seven to thirty days. This imbues the stone with your personal energy. It also permits an attunement to develop, synchronizing your energies with those of the stone, and allowing healing to begin.

When meditating with a stone, you can sit in silent meditation, opening to the stone and allowing any impressions or messages to flow into you. Some people find this frustrating and desire a more guided, active meditation. Alternatively, you can hold the stone during any meditation or shamanic journeying that you do. If you listen to an audiotape, hold the stone during the visualization. I recommend the Elemental Attunement Exercise for anyone in the process of getting to know a specific stone or crystal.

There are some basic concepts to keep in mind when working with any type of crystal. The termination, or the point, indicates the direction of energy flow through a crystal. This is true for any faceted stone. The angles and shape of the facets give direction to the energy. Some people believe that facets also increase the magnitude of the energy. Crystal or other stone balls send out a smoother energy flow in all directions. Finally, crystal clusters tend to radiate group energy. They can bring harmonious energy into a room or a home.

Common Healing Stones

Amber   Purification and protection, patience,
              aids in recovering past-life memories
              and soul fragments; needs to be cleared
              frequently

Amethyst   Catalyst for change, elevates energy to a
              higher level, connection to spirit guidance
              and personal intuition; magnifies energy of
              wearer

Bloodstone   Courage, strength, trust, aids in situations of change

Chrysocolla   Heart-healing, emotional healing, reconnection with Nature, encourages self-esteem and self-love

Citrine   Protection, transforms negative energy, energetic balance, stability, manifestation, clarification; rarely needs clearing

Clear Quartz   General healing, magnifies energy, connection to spirit guidance and personal intuition

Fluorite   Stability, balancing, purification, particularly effective in physical healing; color variations have additional associations

Hematite   Grounding, protection, concentration, mental clarity, transforms negative energy, balancing, cooling and calming

Jasper   Protection, energy balancing and stabilizing; different forms have additional associations

Malachite   Transforming, emotional clarity and healing, balancing, protection, general healing

Obsidian   Grounding, reconnection with Nature, protection, aids with focus and journeying, especially Lowerworld journeys; variations hold additional associations; needs to be cleared often

Rose Quartz   Heart-healing, unconditional love, gentleness, calming

Smoky Quartz Grounding, special ability to ground the spiritual into the physical, protection, stabilizing, dissolves negativity

Tiger's Eye Mental clarity; access to memory, grounding, balancing

Tourmaline Clearing, energizing, transforming, balancing, protection, self-confidence; colored variations have additional Associations

Turquoise Protection, inspiration, strengthening, grounding, aids in communication, connection to spirit guidance, master healer, especially spiritual

When choosing a stone for a specific reason or person, go into the store (or into the field) holding that purpose or person in mind. Send out a request for the ideal stone for that purpose and allow the stone to find you. You may suddenly feel drawn to a stone for no apparent reason. You may walk around the store and keep coming back to that stone.

Sometimes, you will reach for a different stone and the one you need will end up in your hand. Children are wonderful at choosing the best stones for themselves and loved ones. It becomes a game for them. Most children under the age of nine can do this easily without interference from their analytical minds.

Stones, especially those purchased from a store, should be cleared before using them. Stones will pick up energies from their surroundings and impressions from people who have handled them. If a stone had a previous "owner," it may retain some of that person's energies.

Even stones that you have had for a while should be cleared periodically. Some stones, like amber, must be cleared more frequently due to their tendency to absorb negativity. Other stones, like diamond, are notoriously difficult to clear. To make it easier, I recommend frequent clearings.

My favorite ways to clear and purify stones and crystals are smudging with sacred herbs, burying them in earth for seven days, and using running water over them. Burying them and running water over them allow the elements to purify your stones naturally. You might use the water from your sink or spend some time submerging them in a stream. When using any of these purification methods, visualize all unwanted energies breaking up and leaving the stone as you carry out the action of clearing. Continue until you feel the stones are clear and ready to work with you.

Once your stones are clear, you can begin to program them for the specific type of healing you desire. The simplest way to do this is to sit in meditation with your stones and send the intent into the stone. Hold it between both hands and feel the energy of your intent flowing through the stone, filling it. Ask the stone for its assistance in this matter and listen to any messages or thoughts you receive.

Homeopathy

I have used homeopathic remedies since I was a child, and it has worked wonders for our son (and our pets). It is gentle to the system and balances the energy field as it heals. One of the best things about homeopathy is that these remedies taste good—that certainly makes giving a child his medicine a lot easier on a parent.

Homeopathy is an involved discipline requiring years of study to practice it well. However, for the purposes of most parents, we can go about it in an amateur way without worrying about damaging ourselves or our families. It is true that you cannot overdose on homeopathics. I would caution you that some negative effects are rare but possible. The only possible side effect is that the wrong remedy has the potential to create the symptoms it is intended to treat in an individual who does not already exhibit those symptoms. The truth is that this is a rare occurrence and usually the worst that will happen is nothing.

It is true that many homeopathic remedies can be costly. Most of those designed for infants can also create a considerable amount of plastic waste. This is something that many of us have ethical concerns about. However, with an initial outlay to build up an appropriate inventory and to obtain some simple supplies, even the parents of a newborn can treat their baby inexpensively and easily.

To treat an infant, all you need is the appropriate remedy, filtered water, and a glass (preferably dark-colored) bottle with a glass eye dropper. Those "little balls" or tablets dissolve very well in water. Also, since there is no scientifically measurable amount of the remedy in the tablets, you need not be concerned that you will dilute it out by dissolving it in a small bottle of water. Unless you are prepared to get deeply involved with homeopathic education, it is sufficient to dissolve four or five balls, or three tablets, of a remedy in approximately one ounce of water.

Before prescribing any remedy, homeopathic or otherwise, you should look for the cause of your child's discomfort. Often we reach for a pill, albeit a natural one, too quickly before exhausting the other possibilities. Unless the root cause is identified and cleared, you can expect the issue to arise again.

At the end of this section, I have listed several homeopathic remedies and their general uses. Most homeopathic physicians will tell you that the big three for childhood are: *Aconite, Belladonna,* and *Chamomilla.* I recommend that parents purchase a homeopathic reference book. This will help you to determine exactly which remedy is best for your child.

Often a remedy is specific to your child's symptoms, not merely to the condition at hand. For example, the colicky baby who feels better with a little abdominal pressure most likely needs *Colocynthis*. On the other hand, a baby in need of *Bryonia* for colic will be extremely irritable and cannot stand to be moved. Abdominal pressure on a *Bryonia* baby would only result in more screaming.

Shots

For those of you who choose to vaccinate your children, homeopathics are a wonderful way to restore balance, reduce the pain and inflammation of the injection, and prevent many of the adverse reactions that can occur. *Thuja* and *Ledum palustre* can ease much of the pain and worry of vaccinations.

A dose of *Thuja* (preferably 200x) immediately before the injection will prevent the fever and irritability that can follow an immunization. *Ledum* is used for all puncture wounds and can help with pain and swelling at the injection site. Give your child one dose of *Ledum* (12x or 6c) just before the vaccination and another four hours later.

Hiccups

A favorite of ours is the homeopathic series for hiccups. It works wonders for everyone I have tried it on. Our son likes it so much that we keep a plastic bag containing all the hiccup remedies and a small note listing their order in his bathroom.

Begin with one dose of *Aconite* and wait five minutes. If the person is still hiccupping, give one dose of *Arnica* and wait another five minutes. If there is still no relief, try one dose of *Ignatia* and wait five minutes. Follow this with one dose of *Magnesia phosporica* and wait five minutes. If the hiccups are still present, use *Lycopodium*.

Some Homeopathic Remedies for Common Complaints

Acne: *Calcarea sulphurica, Kali bromatum*

Burns: *Urtica urens*

Colic: *Bryonia, Chamomilla, Colocynthis, Magnesia phophorica*

Colds: *Aconitum napellus (Aconite), Belladonna, Bryonia, Ferrum phosphoricum, Pulsatilla*

Constipation: *Alumina, Lycopodium, Graphites, Nux vomica*

Diarrhea: *Arsenicum album, Chamomilla, Colocynthis*

Ear Infection: *Aconitum napellus (Aconite), Belladonna, Chamomilla, Pulsatilla*

Fever: *Aconitum napellus (Aconite), Belladonna*

Headache: *Bryonia, Ferrum phosphoricum, Gelsemium, Natrum muriaticum, Iris* (migraine), *Lachesis* (migraine), *Lycopodium* (migraine on the right side of the head), *Silica* (migraine in the back of the head)

Insect bites/stings: *Apis mellifica, Ledum palustre, Urtica urens*

Injury/Shock: *Aconitum napellus (Aconite), Arnica Montana*

Menstrual Cramps: *Apis mellifica, Belladonna, Chamomilla, Colocynthis, Magnesium phosporica*

Moodiness: *Chamomilla, Nux vomica*

Nausea & Vomiting: *Aconitum napellus (Aconite), Belladonna, Bryonia, Ipecacuanha*

Poison Oak/Sumac/ Ivy: *Urtica urens*

Teething: *Belladonna, Chamomilla, Silica*

Vaccinations: *Ledum palustre, Thuja*

Herbs

Herbs are some of the most common—and most ancient—remedies known to humans. Some pagans use herbs as much as possible, even if only in medicinal teas. Herbal remedies have even made it into the mainstream, now that pharmaceutical companies have decided to certify and market them.

Many of our modern medicines are derived from the chemicals found in plants. Many people believe that herbs are as harmless as homeopathics. It is true that using the whole herb, rather than its derived or synthesized chemical component, is generally more harmonious to the human system. But it is also true that herbs are medicines and can have powerful effects.

Some herbs can be dangerous to certain individuals. For example, goldenseal is a wonderful herb with a wide variety of uses. However, pregnant women and hypoglycemics should not use goldenseal in large doses, even though small amounts may help to relieve nausea during pregnancy. Goldenseal, used over a long period of time, will also diminish the absorption of vitamin B and destroy intestinal bacteria.

It is very important to research the herbs you intend to use, particularly if you are pregnant, breastfeeding, or prescribing for children. Herbs are one case where more is not necessarily better, especially when treating children. Herbs tend to work gently. As a result, you may not see an immediate effect. It is a good idea to start small with children, watching for any signs that the symptoms are improving, before increasing the dosage or switching to another herb.

Rescue Remedy® is one of my favorite things for children, adults, and animals. We have used the cream for burns, cuts, rashes, insect bites, and injections. The tincture is good for just about anything that may cause fear, trauma, or stress. This is ideal to use immediately after a vaccination. Give a couple of drops under the tongue or mixed with water immediately after the injection and as needed for a few hours afterward. Gently rub a little of the cream onto the site of the injection to prevent pain and swelling.

Below I have listed some common childhood complaints and applicable herbal remedies. Keep in mind that echinacea should not be used indefinitely or it loses its effectiveness. At the most, you should use echinacea for eight days on and eight days off, or ten days at one time. Never give honey or tea with honey in it to a child under the age of one year. Honey has been associated with infant botulism, which can be fatal.

Some Herbal Remedies for Common Complaints

Acne: Tea Tree oil; Bach Flower Crabapple; alternate one week each of echinacea/goldenseal tincture, burdock tincture, and red clover tincture

Burns: Cream, gel or liquid of Aloe Vera, calendula, or comfrey root

Colic: Chamomile, fennel, ginger, peppermint teas; for bottle-fed babies, give one teaspoon of tea three times daily in formula or water

Colds: Echinacea/goldenseal; chamomile, sage, ginger teas; bath of chamomile, calendula, rosemary, and lavender

Constipation: Oatmeal cooked in flaxseed tea; licorice tea or tincture; flaxseed oil

Diaper rash: Calendula cream; calendula or chamomile bath; evening primrose oil or lotion; mullein poultice

Diarrhea: Blackberry root syrup, powdered slippery elm bark; goldenseal

Ear Infection: Echinacea/goldenseal; 1-2 drops warm mullein oil in the ear

Fever: Echinacea/goldenseal; tea of lemon balm, chamomile flower, elder flower, peppermint leaf; ginger tea when fever is associated with cold, flu or stomachache

Headache: Chamomile, ginger or peppermint tea; skullcap if the child over six years of age; feverfew for migraines

Menstrual Cramps: Chamomile tea; hot ginger-tea compress; true cramp-bark (*Viburnum opulis*); chamomile and ginger tea bath

Nausea & Vomiting: Aloe vera juice, well-diluted; ginger, peppermint, or licorice root tea; raw honey; barley malt extract; brown rice water

Poison Oak/Sumac/ Ivy: Calendula tincture; aloe vera gel; jewelweed juice (not garden-variety impatiens)

Teething: Clove oil on the gums; licorice root powder paste on the gums; chamomile tea

Vaccinations: Echinacea for three days afterward to prevent or lower a low-grade fever, infection, or irritability

Bodywork

Bodywork is a general word that can mean anything from massage and shiatsu to acupuncture and cranial-sacral therapy. The various forms of bodywork can release repressed issues, keep the energy flowing through the body and maintain the health and vitality of all physical systems. For pagan parents, the most common benefit is pain and stress relief through simple massage.

I understand that this may be an uncomfortable technique to use, particularly with older children and anyone who is not comfortable with physical intimacy. However, it can be a wonderful tool for maintaining both health and an open connection to your children. As parents, we often unconsciously hold, stroke, and touch our children. This comforts them and allows the free flow of loving energy to pass through us into our children.

Many hospitals now offer classes on infant massage, and there are several books available on pediatric massage. This therapeutic massage may include acupressure. There is a Chinese system of pediatric and infant massage called *tui na*. This is a special system of massage that is designed to treat pediatric complaints and diseases.

We used both *tui na* and therapeutic infant massage on our son with wonderful results. Now that he is older, our son still loves to get and give shoulder massages. Rubbing his back when he is tense or feeling poorly helps him to relax and does wonders for his mental state.

Pagan parents can use their own intuitive massage or be guided by their own spirit guides in comforting their children and easing the discomfort of childhood illnesses. Even without a book or any training, parents tend to know instinctively what their children need. And the mere touch of loving hands can work wonders.

Begin by calming and centering yourself. If you can count your child down into a relaxed state of consciousness, this is even better. You might try some of the massage oils on the market that contain therapeutic essential oils. Ask for guidance in helping your child create a healthy body and mind. Allow your hands to take over as you send loving energy through them.

Acupressure is another technique that can also be taught to your children. This is a wonderful tool to teach a child. Rather than asking for an aspirin, a child with a minimal knowledge of this technique can apply pressure between the thumb and forefinger to cure a headache. The applications of acupressure and reflexology are far-reaching.

Diet

Diet is a tough one. Did your children go through the macaroni-and-cheese-only stage? The nothing-but-peanut-butter-and-jelly stage? Or something similar? Most parents I know have difficulties getting their kids to eat what the parents believe they should eat. Sneaking those vegetables or other foods in there can be a challenge, but it is true that many of the common complaints of childhood can be prevented through maintaining a proper diet and a moderate exercise program.

Nutritional supplements and an occasional change in diet can make many chronic conditions more easily managed. A chapter on could easily become at least an entire book on its own. Therefore, I will not write in very much detail regarding specific conditions that can easily be controlled through a change in diet. Suffice it to say that these conditions can be anything from allergies and diabetes to cancer and attention-deficit disorder (ADD).

Many of these conditions often mimic behavioral problems or biochemical imbalances. As a result, a parent might consider having specific tests done if their children show signs of ADD, extreme depression or moodiness, body tremors, and even psychosis.

Speak with your physician or research the symptoms yourself. Special nutritional or blood analyses may indicate a nutritional cause.

Even those conditions that may not officially have their roots in nutrition may be effectively handled with a change in diet. I would also recommend that any new mother who is exhibiting signs of post-partum depression look into the possibility of hypoglycemia. In many cases, diet can be much more important than drugs.

Most pagan parents are very well read when it comes to natural foods. Most of us do our best to keep our families eating well, even if a good number of us also love to indulge in alcohol, desserts and coffee. For those of you that are diabetic or hypoglycemic, it is important to keep in mind that alcohol is a sugar, too. Combining sugar or caffeine with simple carbohydrates or refined foods is an equation that can result in a good deal of suffering.

A well-rounded diet that is low in refined sugars, processed foods, preservatives, and pesticides is a benefit to families for many reasons. Not only does it contribute to a healthy body that is more able to fight off disease, but it also allows us to maintain greater control over our emotions and our energies.

Food allergies, sugar highs, and reactions to preservatives have all been found to affect personality and emotional state directly. Some people even believe that they pick up negative vibrations from animal flesh, particularly if the animal experienced a difficult or painful life and death. Most people in modern society experience varying degrees of reaction to sugar and caffeine.

The path of a priest, priestess, shaman, druid or whatever relies on the individual having complete control over his or her own emotions and behavior. We cannot expect our children to behave calmly and rationally or to gain control easily in Circle if we are feeding them nothing but hotdogs, soda, and chocolate cereal.

Exercise

According to the first-ever *Surgeon General's Report on Physical Activity and Health,* which was released in July 1996, almost fifty percent of Americans between the ages of twelve and twenty-one are not vigorously active on a regular basis. This lack of physical activity increases dramatically during adolescence. It would seem that far too many of our children, at least in the United States, are sitting around, watching television and playing computer games.

It is significant that more than sixty percent of American adults do not achieve the recommended amount of physical activity and twenty-five percent are not active at all. Our children learn from our example and most adults feel that they don't have enough time to work out for themselves, after answering the demands of work and family.

Although many adults are trying to lose weight, most do not enjoy physical exercise, such as sit-ups, jogging, etc. They see this as being time consuming, boring, and physically painful. On the other hand, physical activities like walking, gardening, and playing active games are often viewed as fun and enjoyable.

Fun is the key to getting children to exercise. Parents need to find ways to make it enjoyable for the whole family and set an example by becoming involved with children. Parents care about this for more reasons than simply wanting our children to look good. We care because the benefits of physical activity are substantial.

According to the Surgeon General's report and other studies, regular moderate activity can substantially reduce the risk of developing or dying from heart disease, diabetes, colon cancer, and high blood pressure. Moderate levels of exercise appear to reduce the symptoms of depression and anxiety, improve one's mood, and enhance one's ability to perform daily tasks throughout life. This also helps to keep health care costs down.

Regular moderate activity is important. What this means is that you don't need to introduce your children to the competitive training mindset to achieve these tremendous benefits. You can play, hike, or work around the house with them, as long you do it consistently. Certainly, the benefits increase with the duration, intensity, and frequency of exercise. But the average person can improve his or her health, future, and attitude just by having some fun away from the couch.

Pagan families can experience an additional benefit from moderate exercise. Not only do children have an abundance of energy that may interfere with meditation and ritual, but many adults retain the stresses and tensions of everyday life and work. This can make it difficult to achieve trance states or shut down the mind enough to obtain good results when working with divination or magic.

Exercise and play help to release our tensions and some of the extra energy that may interfere in magical workings. Many pagans find that they are more able to meditate and work effectively in ritual after some form of exercise, partially due to an increase in specific biochemicals called endorphins. Exercise, laughter, and orgasm are some of the best ways to make the body produce endorphins consciously.

Endorphins are biochemical painkillers with a chemical structure like morphine. When they are released, they bind to the opiate receptors in neurons, blocking our experience of pain and increasing our experience of pleasure. They affect the flow of other biochemicals, which play a part in allowing the body to experience altered states.

Endorphins are largely responsible for "runner's high" and that great feeling we get from orgasms. They also have a similar effect as some of the sacred plants used by shamans and other ecstatics across the world. Many people feel as though they are automatically lifted into altered states once their production of endorphins is increased, most notably after exercise.

Exercise can be another tool for pagan families to use to their advantage. Certainly with younger children, it is best to limit the time periods of ritual or meditation. However, these workings may be more productive when following a period of play or exercise.

Energy Work and Colors

As you know, from this book and others, the human energy field is integral to our existence. It permeates the physical body and interconnects us with the universal energy field: that which binds us to All of Life and all worlds. Many of you have heard the phrase "thought precedes action." This is a simplistic way of saying that everything that occurs in the physical realm is caused by events occurring in the purely energetic realms of existence.

What occurs within our energy bodies has a direct effect on the physical and vice versa. Although physical events may have their precedent in the higher energetic realms, physical events are stored and carried by the spirit beyond death and often into the next incarnation. Working consciously with the energy of our families is an excellent way to clear old patterns and memories that may be causing current conditions. It is also probably the best method for creating long-term health.

Pagan families can use the exercises in this book for developing their abilities to feel and see auras. This is an important tool for healing as well. Disturbances in the aura will show up in the physical. They may manifest as emotional or behavioral difficulties or physical problems, including accidents. If you are aware of these disturbances in the early stages, you can begin to work with them before they cause significant problems for your children.

These disturbances will often appear to be discolored or disfigured auras. You may see a dark area or a color that is not quite clear or true. Sometimes, thoughtforms are visible within the energy field of a person. Or, if you are more shamanically inclined, you may perceive these as embedded spirits, insects, or animals. Working with the exercises in this book will provide you the opportunity to develop your own symbolism and ways of seeing accurately.

The easiest way to heal through using energy is to simply channel clear, loving energy to the individual in need. You can do this in a meditation or sit with your hands open toward the person and allow yourself to be a funnel for universal healing energy. Unless you are guided specifically, or well trained, it is best not to direct specific energy or colors to any definite area. Simply offer the energy and let the individual's higher Self direct and use this energy as needed.

If you see disturbances in specific chakras, you may wish to channel the pure color that is associated with the healthy chakra. If the disturbances appear to be an excess of energy in that area, you may prefer to channel the opposite color for a balance. Keep in mind that any energy sent will be used according to the individual choice and best interest. We cannot harm or heal another without their participation or permission on some level of being. Belief plays a large part in both the participation and permission of a patient.

Healthy Colors for the Major Chakras

Base (the base of the spine)
Associated colors: red/black for grounding
Associated body areas: spine, kidneys, adrenals

Sacral/Abdominal
Associated color: orange
Associated body areas: reproductive system,
lymphatic system

Solar Plexus/Belly

Associated color: yellow

Associated body areas: pancreas, stomach, liver, gall
bladder, nervous system

Heart

Associated color: green/pink

Associated body areas: heart, thymus, blood, vagus
nerve, circulatory system

Throat

Associated color: blue

Associated body areas: throat, vocal chords, larynx,
thyroid, lungs, bronchial tubes, alimentary
canal

Forehead/Third Eye

Associated color: indigo

Associated body areas: lower brain, eyes, ears, nose,
nervous system, pituitary gland

Crown

Associated colors: violet/white

Associated body areas: upper brain, pineal gland,
hypothalamus

Breathing

Although the benefits of breath control were discussed
in chapter 3, it is important enough to touch on here as
well. Most biological parents have been though the Lamaze
or Bradley childbirth classes. We know firsthand the importance of regulating the breath during childbirth. Unfortunately, most parents don't think to use this outside of
labor.

The breathing exercises outlined earlier are recommended for anyone in emotional distress or pain. However,

they can require a great deal of focus and concentration that may not be available when a child is hurt. Depending on the age of the child, another technique may be necessary.

Obviously, we cannot do much about the breathing of infants. They don't understand our directions and have not yet regained the necessary control over their physical bodies. Toddlers, on the other hand, respond very well to simple breathing techniques. I have been using "Blow Out the Candles" since our son was approximately two years old, to help him handle the pain of everything from diaper rash to cuts and bruises. Not only does it redirect his focus away from the pain, but it forces his body to relax, even just a little, allowing his endorphins to kick in and reducing both his fear and his experience of the pain. When you cannot redirect your children's attention from the pain, have them blow the "ouch" out rather than blow out the candles.

Older children and teenagers may feel silly with these exercises and should be encouraged to use the breathing exercises in chapter 3. By the time our son was seven, he preferred simple deep and slow breathing for most minor traumas. Keep in mind that you may need to mirror this breathing for them to give them a guide and reminder when they are in pain. Alternatively, older children may be taught a variation on the Lamaze breathing techniques for use after injuries.

"Blow Out the Candles"

In order to use this effectively in a crisis, you may want to practice it with your children when they are not hurt. Use it enough so that when you say "Blow Out the Candles," they will know immediately what you mean.

> Gain your children's attention in whatever non-threatening way you feel is best after an injury or during a time of emotional distress.

Say loudly, (without yelling if possible), "Blow Out the Candles!"

Have your children follow your lead as you take a really deep breath and blow it out strongly. It is important to play this up with younger children. Make faces and silly noises as you suck in a deep breath. Make sure you make noise as you blow out the hardest breath ever to put out all those imaginary candles.

Do not allow children time to get refocused on the crisis. Immediately, tell them that those candles are back and repeat both the deep breath and the exhalation.

Keep this up until the child either cannot maintain the focus or feels better.

Be A Bee

This is similar to "Blow Out the Candles" but is recommended for children over the age of five. It is based on a pranayama technique called *Bhramari*, which translates as "a large bee."

After gaining your children's attention, tell them to Be A Bee. Again, practice will increase the effectiveness of this method in a crisis.

Breathe in deeply through your nose. Breathe out, also through your nose but exaggerate a nasal buzzing or humming sound, like that of a bee.

Repeat for a maximum of three minutes. If necessary, alternate with Breathing Exercise #1 from chapter 3.

Any techniques beyond this can be very involved and it would be a disservice for me to offer you additional or more specific techniques in this section. Your best course of action is to first develop your abilities using the exercises in this book, and then get some training in these methods.

Chapter Six
Family Celebrations

Children love to celebrate!

Of course, the rest of us do, too, but for kids, it's all about the joy of it and not about the planning or cleaning up. Celebrations are magical events for children, and they are a wonderful opportunity to begin to teach children about your particular path. House decorating, singing songs, cooking, and making arts and crafts are all wonderfully interactive methods for introducing pagan ethics and beliefs to children.

The simple act of celebration brings an energy of joy, love, and abundance into your lives. When we celebrate as pagans, we add an energy of appreciation and gratitude that encourages the cycle of blessings to continue. In this way, your family is focusing on the blessings and successes of life. What a wonderful way to guide and empower our children!

Obviously your celebrations will depend on your family and your path. But celebrations need not be limited to "holidays." In our house, we celebrate everything! Sometimes, it seems as though every night is a celebration—which makes it a little difficult to stay on a diet. Other than holidays and the little and big successes of life, we love to celebrate each other. We toast to being together and how blessed we feel to share in each other's lives.

Meals

Mealtimes can become a daily celebration of your family and friends. This allows our children to feel the love and strength of their family each day, even if you only talk in the beginning of a meal before turning on the television. Setting aside even just one meal each week to sit down without distraction and talk to one another is very special.

In modern society, children are too often overlooked and underestimated by adults. Family meals can also become an empowering time when adults are fully focused, at least for a time, on the children's experiences, feelings, and dreams. This makes them feel valued and important—and that builds self-esteem.

Meals at many pagan homes begin with a prayer of thanks. This is particularly true at our home when we are eating meat. Although we have been vegetarians at various times in our lives, we are currently omnivores. As we make offerings to our helping spirits or the fairies or the Spirits of Place, we feel it is equally important to offer back some energy to those who have given their lives that we may eat. The following is one of our prayers that was first published in the summer 1997 issue of *Circle Network News*.

Great Spirit,
We thank You for the gift of this food.
We send blessings of peace, love, and release to all
    whose bodies and energies went into bringing us
    this nourishment.
We honor You in our enjoyment and utilization of
    this meal.
May it bring us health and joy,
    reminding us of our interconnections with All
    That Is.

As we receive, so do we give back
And give thanks for this gift in the Cycle of Life.

The following is a good alternative to use with younger children. It is short, simple, and to the point.

Thank You, Great Spirit.
Thank you, chicken and peas and milk
   (or other food items).
Thank You, Mother Earth.
We love this food.

To cook for another person is a sacred act. Through this act, we provide for their health and pleasure. We also imbue the food with our own energy as we prepare it. I would suggest that you not prepare food for your family during an argument or when you are carrying around destructive feelings. I know that this is not always possible, but you might want to step outside and ground out your tensions into the earth or smudge yourself before beginning to cook.

When you cook or prepare any food for your family, do it with love and that is what they will receive through the food. I make it a habit to charge food, utensils, and cookware with all the prayers I have for my family members while I am preparing anything, even a simple snack. In this way, an everyday meal becomes a powerful means to channel healing and love to our families.

Charging Food

This same exercise can be used to charge anything from cookware to soda cans to crystals.

Taking deep breaths, count yourself down from ten to one.
   Hold your hands out over the food or around the food container.

113

Feel and see loving, healing energy streaming through your hands into the food.

If you have any specific prayers or blessings, direct these through your hands and see them fill the food with their energy.

Paganism is not something we do only on holidays around other pagans. It is a lifestyle that permeates all aspects of life. When we live each day in a spiritual manner, from interacting with co-workers to cooking meals, we attract this beneficial energy and teach our children the beauty of our paths by example.

Celebrating the Holidays

Holidays are great fun and children love the light-hearted importance placed on these special days. One of the easiest ways to teach children about the seasons and the holidays is to create a special family calendar. This is similar to the methods used to teach young children the days of the week and months, as well as the more common holidays. Simply through repetition and having something personal to work with, children learn the relationships between the seasons or the shape of the moon and our holidays. They may also learn of the Deities or other symbols you associate with these holidays.

A Child's Holiday Calendar

You will need:

A piece of cloth in your child's favorite color, approximately 2 feet x 2 feet
A dowel 2 inches longer than the cloth
Needle and thread or sewing machine
String, approximately 3 feet long

Velcro®
Iron-on decorations or fabric glue and extra
      pieces of material
Clear plastic covers or laminating plastic
Index cards

1. Fold a hem at the top of your material and
    sew it along the length of the material, leav-
    ing enough room for the dowel to slip into
    the hem. Do not sew the ends together.
2. Map out your calendar on the material.
    You may want to sketch this out on a piece
    of paper first. You will need a space for the
    month or week of the holiday. Leave room
    for both permanent and seasonal decora-
    tions. For example, a Summer Solstice cal-
    endar might have the week of the solstice in
    the center. A depiction of Summer, the
    Sun, and a particular Deity, animal, or
    plant may be attached above and below
    this with Velcro. Along the outside edge
    may be permanent decorations of your fa-
    vorite symbols, family spirit guides, etc.
3. Attach the permanent decorations. You
    may want to print out iron-on decorations
    or have your children help you paint or
    draw decorations on extra pieces of mate-
    rial. These can then be glued on with fabric
    glue and allowed to dry.
4. Attach one side of the Velcro tabs or strips
    to the center of where your changeable
    decorations will go.
5. Using the index cards, depict the week or
    month of the holiday and make seasonal
    decorations to symbolize the holidays of
    your path or the moon phases. Write the
    name of the holiday at the top of each

decoration card to encourage reading abilities.

6. Laminate these cards or cover them in clear plastic covers. Attach the opposite side of the Velcro to these cards.

7. Insert the dowel into the hem at the top with approximately one inch protruding from either side and tie the string to each end. This will be used to hang your calendar from a nail or doorknob.

8. Hang it up and have fun with it!

Of course, if you are going to have a calendar and begin teaching about the holidays, you will need to follow through and celebrate them in some way. If you have access to a pagan community that includes children in their celebrations, you might consider spending at least a few holidays with them. While family celebrations are powerful and special, pagan children really benefit from sharing this with other pagan children. Not only is it often more fun with other kids around, it also helps them feel that they are not the only pagan kids in the world and that is important.

Planning for family or group celebrations can be as simple or elaborate as you choose. Family celebrations often tend to be more simple and casual but this is not always the case. The first step in creating the atmosphere of a holiday is to decorate the house or family altar. Then there are crafts and activities, party and ritual planning, and anything else you want to include.

Below, I offer you kid-focused ideas for the most common eight neo-pagan holidays plus new moon and full moon suggestions. If your tradition celebrates different holidays, these still may spark your own ideas about ways to have fun with the holidays of your path. You might also want to see *Pagan Homeschooling* (Spilled Candy Publications, 2002) for more ideas and activities.

Winter Solstice

Also known as Alban Arthan or Yule, this is the shortest day of the year and a time of rest between the harvest and planting festivals. From this point on, we move into the light half of the year. Some pagan traditions feel this is when the Veil between the Worlds is thinnest.

Decorations: Evergreens, mistletoe, red and green ribbons, bells, candles, Yule Log, holiday trees, luminarias

Activities: Baking special cookies and cakes, making door wreaths, decorating the Yule log, making bayberry candles, singing carols, decorating a Yule tree, making your own ornaments.

Special Beverages: Eggnog or warm spiced red grape juice

Homemade Yule Ornaments

You will need:

Decorative balls, either Styrofoam or hollow glass (plastic for younger children)
Paint and brushes
Glue
Assorted decorations, such as ribbons, glitter, feathers, colored paper, etc.
Plenty of newspapers and paper towels to cover the space and clean up spills

1. To make glass or plastic holiday balls, remove the hanger from the opening to the ball. Pour in a small amount of your favorite color. Twirl the ball to cover the inside completely or make swirling designs and

allow them to dry. You may add another color once the first color is fully dry.

2. To make Styrofoam holiday balls, paint the ball in your favorite color and allow it to dry. Once the paint is dry, glue on the glitter and other decorations. Objects like small pieces of mistletoe may be stuck into the Styrofoam, but you will want to glue them in if you want to be sure they do not fall off.

Imbolc (*imm-ulk*)

This holiday is also known as Oimelc or Candlemas and celebrates the first stirrings of life within the Earth. In some areas, the first signs of life may be returning in the form of buds on trees or shoots of snowdrops and crocuses.

Decorations: Wheat sheaves and early flowers, red and white ribbons, candles—particularly floating candles

Activities: Making Corn Bride or Brigid Dolls, making and blessing candles, making Brighid's Crosses, preparing the garden for planting

Special Beverages: Hot chocolate

Homemade Candles

You will need:

Paraffin wax or leftover candle stubs
A small pot and a tin can
A box of clean, damp sand
Wicks

1. Hollow out the shape of your candle in the damp sand. If you want your candle to float on water, make it wide and shallow.
2. Place the wax in the tin can. If you are using more than one color, place each color in its own can.
3. Add about an inch of water to the pot and place the can containing the wax in it. Melt the wax in the water over medium to high heat. Do not allow to boil.
4. Place the wick into the center of the sand mold and pour in the wax around it. Be very careful as melted wax can burn your skin. If you want different colors in your candle, allow the first color to cool and solidify before adding the next color.
5. Allow to cool completely before removing from the sand.

Spring Equinox

This equinox is also called Alban Eilir, Eostre's Day, and Ostara. The focus here is often on fertility as well as on balance and harmony since night and day are of equal length.

Decorations: Pastels, eggs, Eostre bunny symbolism, spring flowers, shamrocks

Activities: Coloring eggs, blessing seeds for planting, early gardening

Special Beverage: Ginger ale and white grape juice

Ritual Spring Cleaning

What a wonderful activity to do at this time of year! If you can make it a fun, family affair, you may be surprised at how easily your children join in.

To begin, sit quietly for a moment and guide your children to think back on the year that has passed. Remind them that the year was full of happiness and challenges. Tell them that today, you are going clean away the challenges and fill your home with love and light.

Sings songs as you clear the clutter in your house. Help each other clean rooms, making jokes and tossing trash or socks from across the room. Make it a challenge if you like. The first one done gets a prize. Whatever you do, keep it lighthearted and take breaks when necessary.

Once the clutter is cleared, cleanse the house with smudge, incense, or salt water. Cleanse yourselves first and let the kids have fun with splashing water all over you or smudging your stinky feet.

Then ask for the blessings of your spirit guides and the spirits of the land. Guide your children in a variation on the Egg of Protection from chapter 4 and encircle your home and yard. Fill the Egg with love, protection, and joy.

Beltane

The festival of Bel's Fire may also be spelled *Bealtainne* or *Bealteine*. This is a time of the great marriage between the God and the Goddess and is arguably the most potent fertility festival. Some pagans believe this is the time of year when the Veils between the worlds are thinnest.

Decorations: Mini Maypoles, flowers, God and Goddess images

Activities: Making masks, Maypole dancing, picnics, outdoor bonfires, drumming

Special Beverage: Maywine for Kids—a punch bowl of white grape juice with strawberries and a sprig of woodruff (if you can find it)

Maskmaking

You will need:

Paper plates: cut into half-face mask shapes or
full plates with eye and mouth holes cut
Colored felt, cut into a variety of shapes
Paint and brushes
Decorations, such as glitter, feathers, yarn, rib
bons, etc.
Glue
Twine, elastic string, or Velcro®

1. Imagine the mask you want to make. It may be a personal spirit guide or Deity, a beloved animal or story character, or something from your own imagination. Then choose a plate.
2. Paint it if you want and allow it to dry fully before proceeding.
3. Glue on the decorations to create the mask you imagined and allow it to dry.
4. Attach one end of the Velcro or string to each side at eye level. This will attach at the back to hold the mask on.

Summer Solstice

Also known as Alban Hefin, Litha, and Midsummer, this is the shortest night of the year and a time of rest between the planting and harvest festivals. From this point on, we move into the dark half of the year. This festival has been associated with fairies for centuries.

Decorations: Solar disks, fairy symbolism

Activities: Making solar discs, fairy offerings, camping

Special Beverage: Iced herb tea with honey

A Fairy House

You will need:

Modeling compound or clay that will air dry or
can be dried in an oven
Paint and brushes
Pencil, butter knife, and other tools for deco
rating
Decorations, such as glitter, beads, and flowers
Glue - optional
String - optional

1. Using the clay, create any shape that you can imagine as a fairy house. Some children make it in a shape similar to their own homes. Others make little balls, tree shapes, and flower shapes. Use your imagination.
2. Using the pencil or butter knife, make openings into the house for doors and windows. If you want to hang it up, make an opening to put the string through once the clay is dry.
3. If your clay is air-dry, decorate the house now.
4. If the clay needs to be dried in an oven, do that now. Once fully dry, glue on the decorations.
5. Insert the string, tie, and hang in a special place for your fairy friends.

Lughnasadh (*loo-nah-sah*)

Many pagans use the name Lammas (Loaf-Mass) for this first harvest festival. Historically, this was a time of markets and fairs, games and athletic contests, and meetings.

Decorations: Grains, breads, bright ribbons and banners, sports symbolism

Activities: Baking breads, outdoor games and sporting events

Special Beverage: Alcohol-free beer

Kid Olympics

Well, you convinced your kids to clean their rooms and the house with you on Spring Equinox. Why not create an Olympic-type event for them at Lughnasadh? Using clay or cardboard and metallic paint, you can create medals for each of them. Decorate your yard or a park with brightly colored flags and have plenty of yummy cookies on hand. Then announce the event and have fun with it.

You may want to tailor the events to your children's strengths so that each one wins in at least one event. Or you may want to give each child a gold medal for doing their best. Keep in mind that these events need not be limited to sports. You can include events related to dance, Lego®-building, music, and more.

A story game is always great fun, no matter what other things your children are interested in. Pass out four different words to each child. Have one person start the story using their words. The next person adds to the story, using their four words, and so on until the last person finishes the story using their words.

Autumn Equinox

This equinox also bears the names Alban Elfed and Mabon. It is the second (in some areas, the last) harvest, often the grape and apple harvest. As an equinox, balance and harmony are appropriate focuses for this festival.

Decorations: Apples, grapes, pumpkins, autumn leaves, sun/moon symbolism

Activities: Picking grapes, blessing and storing seeds, decorating with seasonal plants, making   gourd rattles

Special Beverage: Red grape juice

Autumn Equinox Window Leaves

You will need:

Colored plastic wrap
Construction paper
Scissors and glue
String and tape - optional

1. Cut out construction paper in leaf shapes, making sure that you have two matching shapes for each leaf. Leaving a one-half inch to one inch border, cut out the center of each shape.
2. Glue colored plastic wrap to one side of each leaf. Glue the opposite construction paper side on and allow to dry.
3. Optional - make a construction paper tree and tape to a sunny window. Tape your leaves around the tree's branches.
4. Optional - poke a hole in the top and insert the string. Tie and hang in front of a sunny window.

Samhuinn or Samhain (*sow-enn*)

This is the final harvest, also often apples and pumpkins. At this time of year, people and animals are preparing for winter. This is often celebrated as a feast for the dead.

Many pagans believe this is the time of year when the Veils between the worlds are thinnest.

Decorations: Candles, apples, pomegranates, Jack-o-lanterns, gourds, Samhain luminarias

Activities: Apple picking, dunking for apples, making candy apples, hay rides, trick-or-treating, making an ancestor altar

Special Beverage: Warm, spiced apple cider

Samhain Luminarias

Luminarias are sand-filled paper bags that are lit from within by a small candle. While traditionally reserved for the Yule season, they make interesting alternatives to the usual carved pumpkins you see around Samhain. They are also beautiful on directional altars or surrounding a Samhain ritual circle.

You will need:

Paper bags of any color, preferably sandwich-sized
Crayons or paints and brushes
Scissors
Clean, dry sand
Votive or tea candles
Long matches or lighters

1. Decorate your paper bags. If you are using white bags, you can decorate them by coloring or painting images on the bags. Other bags will not show the designs as well. For these, draw the outline of your design on each side the bag and cut it out using the

        scissors. Be sure to place your designs at least two inches from the bottom of the bag.

2. Fill the bottom of each bag with two inches of sand and push the candle slightly into the sand in the center of the bag.

3. Place in a special spot, light, and enjoy!

New Moons

These are times of new beginnings, personal growth, and healing. This is a good time to work with goal-setting. For children, this encourages them to look to the future and make plans to attain their dreams. It also provides an opportunity for more celebration as the next new moon comes around and you can celebrate the successes from the previous month's activity.

To help children learn to set appropriate goals, have them write down (or dictate to you) their greatest dreams and desires. Then write down their goals for the year, the month, and the week or day.

Have them rate their goals on a few questions from 1 to 5, with a 5 meaning "Definitely!" Ask them if the goal is something they look forward to or if it makes them happy. Ask if the goal will help make them better people and if it will help make the world a better place. Ask anything else that you believe will help them choose the right goals for them. Goals with the highest scores should go at the top of the list.

Include grand goals as well as goals you know they will be able to achieve that month. Each small success teaches them that they are winners and that will carry over to the rest of life. But don't discourage them from including goals that are unlikely to be achieved anytime soon. This also teaches them about choosing the best goals for them and about doing what is necessary to achieve their goals in life.

When it comes time to review their goals at the next new moon, celebrate every success, no matter how small. If there are goals that were not achieved, look at the reasons for this. Turn disappointment into a problem-solving or goal reworking exercise and transform the energy of failure into renewed success magic.

Full Moons

This phase brings us the energy of heightening sexuality, psychic influences, emotions, and protection. Many groups get together for drum circles on the full moon. Drumming balances and harmonizes one's energy as it allows for a healthy release of emotion. This is a great activity to share with children at the full moon.

To get things started, play a drum game. This game can include people with rattles, flutes, violins, or those who prefer to use voice or body tapping to share in the rhythms. Play Pass the Rhythm or the Drum Weaving Game. Have one person start with a simple rhythm. They pass the rhythm to the next person in the circle (Pass the Rhythm) or across the circle randomly (Drum Weaving). Continue passing the same rhythm until everyone in the circle has played it least once. Then encourage each new drummer to add their own rhythm to the mix when it is their turn. After a few times around the circle, have the lead drummer play a noticeable change in the beat to signal everyone to play together.

Ritual for Kids

Pagan parents often feel left out of community rituals because children are either not welcome or they are unable to sit through the ritual without disturbing it. For this reason, many families are now organizing rituals specifically designed for kids. When I began to organize kids' rituals in our community in 1999, I was amazed to see how many families wanted to participate in something just for kids. There is a great need for this and if you are at all inclined, I encourage you to explore the possibilities in your area.

The designing of a community ritual for kids does take a bit more flexibility and thought than designing a ritual for one or two of your own children. However, the principles are the same. First and foremost, you need to forget everything you have been taught about what a ritual should be. Creativity and flexibility are the key. While kids' rituals are fun and very casual, this does not mean that the importance of the ceremony is lost. It's just different.

Teens and many older children enjoy formal, structured ritual. These children do not need a special ritual written just for them, but it is an excellent idea to let them write their own or contribute to the design of one. At this age, they may be seen as priests and priestesses in training, if that is their choice. Designing rituals that are meaningful to them is an empowering act that encourages their innate spirituality and creative abilities to flow through.

Younger children are the ones we need to consider most when creating rituals for kids. They need something a bit more fun and freeform. To force them to sit through a long, involved adult ritual will teach them nothing and will bore them to whining. No one wins in a situation like that. But in an age-appropriate ritual, they learn a great deal about the ceremony, the value of ritual, and about themselves.

So let's start with the basic outline of ceremony. You have an Opening, a Ritual Core, and a Closing. Adult ritual will expand on each of these to create more ritual elements for a more complex ceremony. For kids' rituals, these three are all you need.

In your Opening, you will want to create sacred space and call in the blessings of your spirit guides and Deities. Think of this in terms of the age of your kids and you will gain some insight into how to do this. When you have an outline ready, ask them to help you fill in the details and you will be impressed with the natural spirituality that comes through.

For many neo-pagan groups, the creation of sacred space involves casting a circle. Circles can be cast in many unique ways. You might try singing a circle song to cast your circle. Your children may appreciate a short visualization of a bubble or a circle of stars surrounding you. Or you may enjoy passing a simple but powerful sentence around the circle. To do this, have the ceremony leader turn to the person on his or her left and say, "From my heart to your heart, we stand in strength." Each person passes that on until it reaches the leader and the circle is cast.

Many groups cleanse their circles by sweeping with the besom (Witch's broom), smudging, or consecrating with salt, water, or corn meal. These are simple and fun ritual elements that children tend to enjoy doing. Just warn those attending that they may get soaked when your two-year-old drenches them with water using her evergreen branch at the next Yule ritual.

Calling in the blessings of your spirit allies can be one of the most fun parts of kids' rituals. It may help to let the children decorate the main altar and four directional altars. The things they come up with are wonderful. I remember at one ritual, local children had bubble liquid and wands on the East altar, fire Pokemon® on the South altar, a Beta fish in a tank in the West, and loads of rocks and dirt at the North. Of course, each altar also held an appropriate stuffed animal. It was fantastic!

With very young children, an adult may want to do the speaking while the child lends his or her energy to the invocation. All children can assist through directional symbolism. We've used bubbles, sparklers, water guns, and seed throwing to include children and help remind them of the energies being invoked.

When children begin to help with invocations, the calls should be simple and short. Make it a safe space where everyone can mess up a line, erupt in giggles, or decide they are too shy to participate this time. Adults should be prepared to act as backup if a child suddenly gets shy.

Songs and chants can help eliminate the pressure to perform that can be felt when a child has a solo speaking part. Simple chants, like "Earth, Air, Fire, Water: Come in, Come in, Come in!" can be shared by everyone. Many families prefer for older children and adults to invoke the God and Goddess or Spirits of Place, but this is certainly personal preference. If you have younger children, why not ask them how they would invite in these Deities and see how they can help?

The core of the ritual should also be kept shorter and sweeter the younger your children are. The truth is that even older kids can lose the ritual focus during a long, involved central portion. The core is the reason for the ritual; the ritual action. The suggested activities above for each of the eight holidays are nice additions to the core, provided you can maintain the ceremonial energy. For example, dancing a Maypole or walking a labyrinth of Winter Solstice luminaries are excellent for this portion of children's rituals.

The Closing serves to return everyone to mundane consciousness. This should be done as a reversal of your Opening, making sure to thank all the spirits that were invited. Children appreciate the clarity of a Closing and you might want to end with "This circle is now open."

The real key to family celebrations is to make them reflect your family. Outlines and rituals from books or local groups are excellent to use as references or starting points. But just as your family is unique and growing, so should your celebrations and family rituals be dynamic and flexible in order to serve your family's needs best. Remember that no matter what form your celebrations take, the fact that you are honoring each other and the joy in life will renew the love and strength of your family. These are the special times that children remember and want to recreate with their own families when they grow up.

Chapter 7
Children and the Community

What does "community" mean to you? Is it those people living in your neighborhood, the people you work or go to school with, or those people who you hang out and play with? Most of us participate in more than one community at any given period in our lives. We have our local or neighborhood communities, our work communities, and the communities defined by any clubs or special interest organizations we may belong to. Children are usually an integral part of most of our communities, but they also have their own groups, exclusive of adults. These generally include such "communities" as sports teams, neighborhood friends, and other special interest groups.

While most pagans also participate in multiple communities, their identities are often quite different depending on the community. This is certainly true to some degree for all people, but pagans have the added component of their religions. The majority of us are closet pagans, at least in some of our communities. And unfortunately, our spiritual communities often do not coincide with our neighborhood or work communities.

This can make things difficult for both pagan parents and their children. Within a community, our children learn the behaviors that are acceptable to that society. They also begin to learn who they are through the mirrors of their community members. Parents are responsible for teaching and guiding their children through the complex web of relationships and acceptable behaviors specific to that group.

While each community has its own particular flavor and ethical values, the mainstream community tends to be very different from the pagan community. While we may wish for the ideal world where we can all live together in diversity and harmony, pagan parents and children walk a tightrope of social values. It can sometimes be a challenge for a young pagan to avoid bleed-through of social values from one community into another.

Most pagan families want their children to feel comfortable with the human body and with both intimacy and sexuality. We all encounter a majority of humans that are afraid of sexuality and nudity. Most of these people carry similar fears regarding simple intimacy and "alternative" sexual preferences.

As pagan parents, we hope that our children will honor themselves as well as each other and the Earth. We dream of them walking this lifetime in spiritual connection with All of Life. But this is another area where our children are likely to encounter truly saddening and frightening variations in belief.

The behaviors and ethics of pagan communities will obviously differ to some degree from those of the mainstream. It is important that pagan parents recognize this as we are supporting the development of healthy, balanced identities in our children. We may need to make it clear to younger children who running around the neighborhood naked is neither a good idea, nor is it always safe. The subject of pagan and mainstream identities will be discussed in greater detail in the chapter on Honesty versus Secrecy.

Any community is not truly a *community* unless it fulfills specific needs for all its members. A community exists to bring people together to meet common goals. We need not all be pals in a community, but we do need to know that if we need help, we are not alone. Community members pull together when someone is injured or has lost a loved one or is in need of an operation they cannot afford.

Pagan community members have contributed to court cases for other pagans wrongly accused of a variety of things, mainly related to their alternative religion. Pagans have banded together to clean up parks and riverbanks and to speak out against discrimination or harassment. We have come together magically to support someone through a difficult emotional time, to send prayers and energy to help someone pass an important test or get into a certain college, and to aid the police in stopping a serial criminal.

But communities need to be there when a crisis is not going on, too. It is with our communities that we share our thoughts and feelings. These are the people who are there when a baby is born, a child reaches adulthood, or a wedding takes place. They are our babysitters, our rides to events, and the people we go out to the pubs with. We share the good times and the bad with these people, and we all grow through the experience.

This is the essence of community. The strength of our communities is vital to our survival and well-being. A strong community becomes a type of extended family for many people. This is an essential need for our children, who are the future of our communities and of our world. Children need a community to help them feel connected and a part of something.

Even in mainstream culture, it is a fact that the modern family is going through some very difficult changes. Many people do not live near their extended families. Many do not even have contact with everyone in their nuclear families. When the contact is present, it is often strained by a lack of honest communication as well as other factors.

For pagans, there can be an even greater need for a spiritual family. Many pagans have either not informed their biological families of their spirituality or they were rejected by family because of their choice of religion. They are left without the one institution that is supposed to be supportive always and love you unconditionally: the family. As a result, more and more pagans are looking to their spiritual communities to fill the roles of family.

Pagan Communities

Many of us seek out pagan community for our children. Whether we are new to paganism or have been solitary for years, we want our children to be able to interact with a community that is welcoming and supportive of our beliefs. We don't want our children to grow up always needing to be careful what they tell to whom. Whether one follows a Druid, Wiccan, or Asatru path, we want our children to feel safe being open about their spiritual beliefs.

As parents and guardians, we recognize that children need the company of their peers. They need to be able to play with others of their own age. They need to be able to talk about life and develop their own identities and get into trouble—all with other children. This is another major reason why pagan parents often decide to become involved with some type of pagan community.

As a child raised pagan at the beginning of the "New Age" movement, I always wished for friends my own age at metaphysical gatherings and seminars. Although I was included in everything my mother did and I was accepted by the new leaders of the movement, it was very clear that I was the only child. Rarely did we encounter other children, and this was difficult for me at times.

As a result, it has been very important for me to seek out other pagan families and communities that might provide our son with peers and friends within a spiritually safe space. I find this to be the case with most pagan parents I meet. Many individuals who once resisted involvement in a group will actively search for one when they have children.

Since children will develop energetic bonds to trusted adults, we need to be aware of the group dynamics in any community. Covens and Groves can become a child's family. We spend a considerable amount of time together. These are the people who attend and perform Namings and adulthood ceremonies. We share all the festivals with them, and we are both emotionally and energetically open to them in Circle.

These people are not always blood family. Therefore, more than most blood relatives, they can simply walk away from the group. This can leave the children in these groups feeling abandoned. In groups with a high degree of transition, children can suffer soul loss and energetic damage.

My intention here is not to recommend against involvement with these intense types of groups. My point is simply this: be aware and exercise restraint and wisdom when involving your children with a new "family."

When a group breaks up or a special member leaves, treat it as a type of death. Recognize that there will be grief that needs to be expressed. This grief will often be accompanied by a variety of other emotions, just as in a physical death. There may be anger, feelings of abandonment or guilt, deep sorrow, loneliness, and a multitude of other feelings that all need to be freely experienced in a safe space.

On the other hand, these types of communities can provide a necessary extended family and support to parents and children alike, even if they do not include other pagan children, as long as the children are honored and treated with respect within the group. These are the communities that teach our children, through word and action, that they are important and valued members of that community.

This is a tremendous benefit to the pagan child involved with any pagan community. Too often in modern society, children are "just kids" and as such are treated as annoyances, restrictions, or as unintelligent second-class citizens. We ignore them and pacify them with television, food, and video games.

Children are rarely included in decision-making or creating community. However, they receive a great deal of the blame when they begin to get into trouble and act out of their soul loss and energetic blocks. They are labeled as "at-risk" or bad kids, and we often blame their parents—who are frequently lacking any real community support or involvement—for their actions.

This is not the reality in most pagan communities. Certainly, our children get into trouble, but we tend to handle it differently. We ourselves remember doing much of what they do. Some of us still do it, whatever it may be. But most of us treat it as a process of growth rather than as a sign that we have bad kids who need excessive discipline and punishment. Discipline is balanced with love and encouragement. Most children (that I know) who have been raised pagan with some form of pagan community are considerably more respectful and responsible than other children.

Festival Communities

The neo-pagan movement has spawned a series of extended "family" communities based around the various festivals held across the country. While many pagans do restrict themselves to regional gatherings, there are a large number who travel from coast to coast. These are often pagan speakers and vendors who generally travel individually but hook up with the rest of their magical family at communal house gatherings or campsites.

Children of festival families are often treated as our own. While children are usually given a greater degree of freedom at festivals, largely because they are safer spaces, nearly everyone in the community keeps an eye on them. A child cannot get hurt or lost at a pagan festival without many people coming to his or her rescue.

Furthermore, anyone who dares to harm a child in any way, at a pagan festival, will answer to the greater community, whether we know the child or not. There is zero tolerance for this type of behavior at pagan festivals. Even if an individual is merely suspected of harm to a child, they can count on being watched very carefully.

Most festivals have some form of childcare or kid's track of workshops and games designed specifically for younger pagans. Not only does this allow parents to attend workshops and interact with other adults, but it also provides a safe space for children of varying pagan paths to play together and make friends without having to hide their spiritual beliefs.

These children's and teen's tracks have become very popular at many festivals. They serve several purposes. First and most obvious, they provide a forum for our children to learn about other paths from known and respected practitioners. This encourages them to explore and define their own spirituality. It also frequently gives them the opportunity to meet with well-known pagans, such as authors, elders, and other community leaders.

Perhaps more importantly, these events empower our children. Children are not simply expected to go off to play so that the adults in the community can do their thing. They are encouraged to learn and do what the adults are doing, without having to attend "adult" classes. Many children, even teens, do not feel the adult classes are always applicable. Furthermore, they don't want to do things always with Mom or Dad.

In many cases, children are encouraged to share what they have learned, often through creating and offering their own rituals to the community. This can go a long way to developing community interaction and leadership skills, as well as supporting the healthy development of ego and self-confidence. It also provides our children with a format within which they can express themselves as they see fit and not merely from within the framework of family or tradition.

Festivals are most definitely the times when all pagans can freely and openly express themselves. These are the safe spaces where we feel comfortable just being whomever we feel we are or whomever we choose to be at the time. Pagan parents must keep in mind that their children will be exposed to all this wondrous diversity at a pagan gathering, particularly at the outdoor festivals.

This is the reality of many pagan festivals. Of course, the nudity is not generally in evidence at the indoor festivals, but the variation is still very present. While this is freeing and spiritual to most, it can be intimidating or even frightening to many, especially if it is one's first pagan festival.

Those parents who are not comfortable with nudity, sexuality, body piercings, tattoos, men in skirts, or a wide variety of wild outfits would be well advised to avoid the outdoor festivals and be cautious about hotel conferences. These parents might prefer to find a metaphysical or pagan community in covens, meditation groups, Groves, or even churches, such as the Unitarian Universalist church.

Many of those who were not raised in a pagan family grew up with the indoctrinated beliefs that are prevalent in mainstream society. Even if we have chosen consciously to reject these beliefs, they are often still present and can act to color our reactions and our perceptions. This is often the case among pagans attending their first festivals.

Sexuality is possibly one of the most emotionally charged subjects in modern society. These feelings do not automatically change once one realizes that he or she is pagan. Pagan individuals and events can bring all of our sexual and body image fears, hang-ups, and judgments to the foreground.

At any type of pagan gathering, large or small, you are likely to come face to face with people of varying sexual preferences. As a result, new pagans are constantly offered the opportunity to handle any indoctrinated beliefs or lingering judgments they may have regarding certain sexual preferences. I have yet to meet a pagan who does not support another's right to sexual preference and lifestyle.

Pagans are normally very accepting of the personal expressions of others. So, whether you choose to go naked, robed, or proudly display body piercings and tattoos, we support your right to choose and freely express yourself, provided you do not harm anyone and are responsible for your actions. Many pagans believe that they are not only expressing their freedom from limiting and unhealthy societal morals by being naked, but they deeply feel that this brings them closer to Nature, their spirituality, and their Deities.

Some pagans feel that being skyclad in their rites and celebrations is asked for or required of them by their Gods. Others have the exact opposite beliefs: that their Gods will be offended if ritual participants are not appropriately clothed. And of course, most pagans are somewhere in the middle of these two belief systems.

I am not going to say that there are no judgments on both sides of the nudity issue. I will say that one of the beautiful things about pagans is a widespread refusal to dictate the attitudes, beliefs, or behaviors of other pagans. We have had enough of that from the majority culture. We will not do it to our pagan brothers and sisters. I would only hope that, as pagan parents, whether you choose to experience these events or not, that you would encourage your own family to continue the important pagan tradition of supporting each other in the right to choose.

The festival ideal is that you may do as you wish, provided you harm no one. The reality is that separate sections have been created within some of the larger festivals for things like quiet camping or clothing required. The childcare area, if present, is almost always a clothing-required space. This has come as the result of our differing beliefs and feelings regarding the various freedoms at pagan events.

Not all pagan paths require, or even permit, nudity in ritual. Not all agree on the monogamy/polyamoury issue. And not all agree on the wearing of ritual garb outside of ritual. But while we all do support the choices of other pagans, not all of us feel comfortable in that space and not all of us want our children exposed to all that can mean.

It is our responsibility, as parents, to decide what we feel is beneficial and appropriate for our children. If you were not raised pagan, I would recommend that you spend some time considering this before deciding to head off to the summer festivals. If your children are old enough, you may want to include them in a discussion about these subjects and find out how they feel.

Many children (like many adults) have body image issues. As children reach puberty, these issues are compounded by all that chaotic energy and rampaging hormones. Sexuality and appearance become extremely important. Therefore, it is normal for a child, particularly one whose family is new to all of this, to feel initially uncomfortable at an outdoor festival.

Most parents try to empower their children to think for themselves with wisdom. Within reason, pagan families tend to allow children to decide for themselves what is comfortable attire at a festival. However, if you have limitations for children under a certain age, it is very important that you make those restrictions clear to your children up front. Things can feel very loose and free at a festival. Children need to know if there are boundaries, and they need to be very clear what those boundaries are.

Festival communities can provide a necessary support system for children in the absence of an extended pagan-friendly family or a coven, grove, temple, etc. This is particularly true when the family returns to the same festival year after year. A type of social structure will evolve among the children during a festival that can be similar to a school or neighborhood community.

All the usual dynamics are present in these festival communities, from sexual tensions and dating to competition and trouble-making. However, there is the additional element of spirituality. These children will often make long-term and long-distance friends at festivals largely because they share what is often perceived to be a mainstream social stigma. They all belong to the same underground or minority society, and this brings them together for a common purpose.

The festival community also brings together people of all age groups for a common purpose. This environment has even greater potential than do groves, covens, etc., in creating a bond between the generations. Elders are very much a part of the festival community. They are honored and respected in many ways. This is an important attitude for our children to develop. Attitudes regarding the elderly in modern, mainstream society are frightening and saddening.

Pagan children are exposed to a community where elders are valued for their perspective, power, and life experience. Both generations have the opportunity to interact and to learn from each other, empowering both the young and the old. Our elders are able to share their knowledge and experience, while gaining a feeling of inclusion and respect. In return, our children learn about life and spirituality from those who have been around for a very long time. The Old Ways are passed on, giving everyone a feeling of continuity and connectedness.

Parental awareness and interest are vital components in the relationships our children have with community. If we pay attention, listen to our children, and observe carefully, we will be more likely to catch potential problems before they get out of hand. More than that, we remind our children every day that they are our top priority and that we are available for support, guidance, protection, and simple venting.

If we, as parents, can wisely walk a strong and sensitive path within our communities, we truly honor each other and ourselves. We learn from each experience and hopefully, bring that new understanding into our homes and our relationships with our families. We then become the type of parent most of us would like to be. Our children may still argue with us, but they will certainly respect us as honest, strong, spiritual beings who love them very much.

Chapter 8
Handling the Tough Questions

I would like to preface this chapter by saying that, even if I had a Ph.D. in child psychology and another in family relationships (which I don't), I still could not be an expert on what is right for your family. What I offer you is based on my experience and my academic and spiritual training: please do not accept these as the Way It Must Be. Rather, use this chapter as a guide and a catalyst for deciding what is best for your family, recognizing that your truths may change with time, too.

When you speak of parenting, you must consider the questions that inevitably arise with children. The fact is that most of these questions are tough because we are not really sure of the answers ourselves or we retain limiting beliefs about the answers. How does a parent discuss sex with a child when he or she is not fully comfortable with nudity, sex, or intimacy? How do we answer questions about what happens when someone dies when we aren't really sure and are afraid to die ourselves? And how do we guide them through their relationships when we still have difficulty with ours?

The first course of action is to recognize that each parent is human. We are all still growing and learning. It is our responsibility to educate ourselves as best we can. But we can only work with what we have available to us at any given time. The answers a parent gives at one time may change as they learn more and gain more experience. It is okay to say that we do not know. Better to be honest with our children than to lie to them by pretending to be more than we are.

The answers to these questions will vary according to the child's age, family tradition, and the parent's personal beliefs. However, I can give an overview of the general pagan and metaphysical beliefs about most of these issues here. I will certainly miss some questions. It could take an entire book to answer the really big questions fully and even then, we could not possibly come up with every difficult issue that may be raised.

I can suggest only that you trust your intuition and be as honest as possible without inflicting harm. If you do not know the answer, let the child know that you will find out—and then do so. Be sure to frame your responses according to the child's age and comprehension or emotional level. Be supportive and understanding of their responses and make it clear that you are there if they need you.

What happens when you die? Where do you go?

As a pagan parent, you can say that pagans recognize the cycles of life in all things. We celebrate the seasonal cycles and honor the death and rebirth in our world. All pagans believe that the spirit continues after death. Some of us believe in a form of reincarnation, and some of us do not. But we all believe in the possibility of contact with the departed after death; that life and love continue without a physical body. We also believe that spirit guides or Deities are with us once we leave this body to guide us safely Home.

144

Many pagans believe that the free soul, or astral body, travels about during sleep. During this time, we have access to other dimensions and other beings. We may very well carry on relationships with departed loved ones while our physical bodies sleep. This is probably the best way to explain this to young children.

Toddlers are just not ready for an in-depth discussion of the spirit versus the body. They may be able understand that a loved one's body has died but that this person still lives in the Dreamtime. In a way, they have just moved to live in another place, without their body. We can still see them, especially when we are dreaming.

To answer this question honestly, you need to decide what you believe about the Afterlife. That can be a difficult thing to do, and I recommend doing it before your children start asking. You might also consider explaining the different beliefs around the world. Visiting a church, synagogue, Buddhist temple, and high priest or high priestess is often beneficial for older children.

Because death is such an involved and highly charged area, I would suggest that you explore some of the recommended reading books that are listed in the back of this book.

Will you ever die? Will I die? What would you do if I died?

It is best to be as honest as possible when faced with this question. The truth is, all of our physical bodies will die eventually. The important point is that we have all died before and will probably die again, if you choose to believe in other lives. The Other Worlds are not unfamiliar territory. We merely lose access to those memories in this reality due to limitations of mind and body.

Many children under the age of five appear to have a casual attitude about death. It is so much like sleep that they cannot fully comprehend that loved ones will not return. They are just not old enough to realize that physical death means that body is gone forever. Be aware that discussions of reincarnation at this age may result in the child's assumption that the physical body will come back to life.

During the elementary school years, children recognize death as a permanent condition. They also learn to fear it as more than a separation from friends and family. In our modern society, children fear that they will simply end or be completely alone or have a painful death.

It is rarely a good idea to lie to a child. Parents do not want to promise something we cannot guarantee that we will be able to keep. Imagine how your child would feel at your funeral after you had promised never to die. How easy might it be for this child to trust again?

Our son has been through the death of pets and, as a wildlife rehabilitator, death is a common part of life around here. He has not yet experienced the death of a human loved one, but we talk about this from time to time. He knows that we have made sure he will be taken care of if we die while he is young. He's seen our wills, and he chose the people who will be his legal guardians if that becomes necessary. Whenever we say, "I'll always be here for you," we follow that up with "...whether I am in my body or not." The thought of it certainly causes sadness, but he has a deep understanding that we will never really leave him and that our spirits will always love him.

As for what you would do when asked if your child will die and what would you do if he or she does, be "as honest as possible without causing harm." Harm in this case may be telling a child that your life would be over, that you would be utterly devastated and would never recover should they pass over. Not only does this place a tremendous amount of responsibility on the child, responsibility that is not within their conscious control, but it does not reinforce any assertion you may make that life and love continue after physical death.

What happens if I kill myself?

The answers to this question will largely depend on exactly what the child means by "what happens." Few modern pagans believe that a soul is relegated to an eternity of suffering for taking one's own life. On the other hand, if the child is asking what you would do in this situation, you must answer accordingly.

If the child wants to know what happens to the soul after a suicide, it is important to find out why. This child may merely be interested. However, we cannot ignore the possibility that the child is either looking for attention or is honestly considering taking his or her own life. In any case, explain the spiritual effects as you understand them and be aware of any other warning signs from this child or others in your family. A child may ask because they have heard a friend, sibling, or other family member speaking about suicide.

In my shamanic travels, I have not experienced that those who have committed suicide go to any form of Hell, other than perhaps a Hell of their own creation, depending on their beliefs. For a time after death, we experience reality based on the beliefs we held in the previous incarnation. Someone may indeed create a Hell or other difficult situation if his or her beliefs are strong enough. For the most part, these people meet up with guides and go through the same process as any other departed spirit.

The cold, hard truth is that suicide does not eliminate one's problems. If you believe in reincarnation, it may postpone it until the next life, but you just have to handle it all over again. It may also be difficult for a spirit to fully release from this reality if there is unfinished business or if the spirit feels he has made a mistake in taking his own life.

The child who asks what you would do if he or she committed suicide is also begging for attention and help. It is not worth the risk to assume that the child is merely looking for attention. To ignore this could mean missing or denying vital warning signs. It could also send an attention-seeking child into a real depression or rebellion that may result in death. If this is a possibility in your home, call a suicide hotline or speak with your doctor or counselor.

Do animals have spirits?

The answer to this is an absolute yes. I don't know of too many people today, pagan or not, who would disagree. It has been my experience that animals experience similar death processes to humans. They reincarnate and they tend to forget other lives while they inhabit a body. They may be spiritual guides for their people, on both sides of the Veil, and they may have their own spirit guides who show up after death.

Some people may argue that animals are only part of a group soul. I would have to disagree, based on my experience and the experience of other deathwalkers I have known. In a way, we are all part of a group soul. We are all interconnected at some level of being. This does not preclude the existence of an individual soul and its personal development.

Where do babies come from?

This should probably be handled from a purely physical point-of-view first. Everyone who is nearing the age when they are physically capable of getting pregnant or impregnating a woman should know the basics of anatomy and conception. Most pagans agree that our children should also be educated in contraceptive methods. If a sexually uneducated child becomes pregnant or impregnates someone else, then the parents have failed in their jobs.

There are a number of good books, for all ages, on the market today that deal with these topics. The age and comprehension level of the child should dictate an appropriate conversation. Many pagan children have seen plenty of naked bodies. This is natural and healthy, within the pagan belief systems. These children are well aware that there are differences between the male and female bodies. This generally makes descriptions a little easier.

We need not fear that our descriptions will lead to sex or pregnancy. Kids who will experiment will do it whether we talk to them or not. Curiosity is natural and healthy, within reason. We are not better parents if we cling blindly to the dream that our children are innocent, asexual cherubs. Just as we demand all the facts in order to make the best decisions for ourselves and our families, we owe it to our children to provide them with the tools necessary to make their own intelligent, informed decisions.

As pagans, we tend to be much more open and natural with our sexuality. We recognize that our children are often sexual beings at a much younger age than the usual age of consent. While few of us encourage our children to become sexually active at any age, we are intelligent enough to realize that this possibility exists. We do them a disservice if we close off all communication related to this and pretend that they won't consider it until they are legally adults or married.

It is important that our children feel comfortable enough to come to us if they need to talk about sex or possible pregnancy. We need to be able to handle this with maturity. Since many neo-pagans were not raised pagan, I strongly recommend that you work with your own beliefs and feelings regarding sex. It is not a subject that is easily avoided in pagan communities. Our children and our societies will benefit greatly if they can grow up without the multitude of hang-ups and fears surrounding sexuality that the previous generations did.

As far as where babies come from on a spiritual level, this will depend on your personal beliefs. You may want to discuss reincarnation or concurrent lives with your children. You may want to use this as an introduction to the cycles of life and what happens after death. As always, keep in mind the age and comprehension level of the child.

Can I have a baby?

As we all know, there is a big difference between can and should when it comes to having and raising children. From a pagan perspective, we are manifestations of the God and Goddess. Sexuality and procreation are sacred gifts. However, they are gifts that must be enjoyed with honor, respect, and intelligence. Anything less minimizes the blessings and does nothing to benefit our total soul growth.

If your children are still living with you, this is not a decision that they make alone. This will impact the entire family. This is something that parents may want to discuss without the children before they reach puberty. Everyone needs to know what you are and are not willing to tolerate. You need to be clear on your reactions and decisions if a child should come home and say "I am/My girlfriend is pregnant."

This is also something that should be discussed along with contraception if you suspect that a child may be sexually active. Unless it is a personal decision, most pagans support abortion rights. While some may decide this is not right for them, they will almost always support the right of another to choose their own path.

Whatever your decision, keep in mind that your child may decide on a different course of action. This is something else that should allow open communication so that our children feel comfortable coming to us with these issues. We do not want them to feel alone or backed into a corner. Children having children must be a family decision (if at all possible), with full family support.

My boyfriend/girlfriend wants me to have sex. What should I do?

This is a question that goes beyond the mere act of sex in a relationship. It encompasses the self-esteem, self-confidence, and personal strength of a child. Each of these areas will need support no matter what the decision is.

The child may or may not want to become sexually active. This question does indicate a feeling of being pressured. The child may fear that the fate of this relationship may depend on sex. Sex given in this way does not honor the God and Goddess, the relationship, or one's Self. Pagans may appear at face value to place a high emphasis on sex and, to be honest, many do. But no one who follows an Earth-based religion or spiritual path would respect a pressured or forced sexual encounter.

Since sexuality is viewed as sacred (and fun) to pagans, it is important that it be done right. Consenting adults may do as they please, but it is important that our children grow up without fears and issues surrounding their sexuality. These issues often lead to body image problems, lower self-esteem and confidence, and the attraction of unhealthy relationships throughout one's life.

Your reactions to this may vary according to the actual and emotional age of the child. Sexuality involves much more than one's physical body. At its highest and most beautiful, sex can activate all of the energy centers of both people, clearing the aura, and bringing both energy systems into complete harmony at the highest levels of Self.

Unfortunately, sex can also create unhealthy energetic bonds and cause auric damage, depending on the situation. This plus the multitude of physical conditions a person may contract through sexual intimacy are valid reasons for education and a good deal of thought before making any decisions.

Without unnecessarily limiting beliefs, judge for yourself what is behind the question. Is the child afraid of losing his or her partner? Does he or she want to become active but is nervous or afraid for some reason? And most importantly is this child ready to handle being sexually active?

What if I told you I was homosexual/bisexual?

In most cases, this is not a big issue in pagan families. Alternate sexual lifestyles are as accepted as any other lifestyle that may be common among pagans. However, parents may have surprising reactions, whether they were raised pagan or not.

Sometimes, parents will fear for the difficulties that may lie ahead for a homosexual or bisexual child. While the desire to protect children from the hardships of life is admirable, we cannot protect them from their own learning experiences. In addition, our reactions and expectations of difficulty may contribute to our children's beliefs and fears, making things even more difficult on them.

Occasionally a parent may be supportive while feeling sorry for themselves with regard to the possibility of grandchildren. Keep in mind that homosexuality and bisexuality do not preclude the possibility of children. Sexual preference does not necessarily prevent people from adopting, if they should choose to. There are also plenty of homosexual and bisexual people with their own biological children. It should also be noted here that heterosexuality does not guarantee grandchildren.

As parents, our main concern must be with the health and happiness of our children. While many people may not want to admit it, even to themselves, there remain lingering beliefs and fears about alternate sexuality deep within their subconscious. It may be perfectly fine for other people and you may have several homosexual or bisexual friends, but to have it within your own family is not acceptable. You may even be very supportive of your child, but there is a nagging discomfort or uneasiness about it.

Repressing these feelings is not healthy for anyone, and your child may pick up on them psychically, particularly if the two of you are close. It is important to be honest about your feelings while supporting your child. It is also important to work to clear these limiting beliefs so that you can unconditionally love and support your child in all of his or her choices.

You might also remember that this is not a choice any more than one chooses to be heterosexual. It is not something that can be cured or cleared or changed. Individuals may deny their sexual preference their entire lives to make other people happy, but this does not mean they are heterosexual. It also does not mean that our children are happy.

Why are you homosexual/bisexual?

This is probably more difficult than the previous question. If your child is asking this, there is a good possibility that to the outside world, you were once heterosexual. You may have been married to the child's other parent.

If your child has never known you to be heterosexual, it is likely that there is no feeling of betrayal or resentment involved in the question. A child certainly recognizes when his or her family differs from the majority. A child may need to know the realities of sexual preference and it is best they hear it from you to get an accurate understanding.

There is always the possibility that this question is the result of taunting from peers and other members of the community. If you are openly homosexual or bisexual, just as if you are openly pagan, you may want to consider being open to questions within reason, not because it is anyone's business, but because most people who have not experienced it cannot really understand it. And ignorance is often dangerous.

If you are willing to discuss this with your child's friends and their parents or with teachers, you have the potential to do a lot of good. Not only do you make things easier on your children, but you also pave the way for others who may be too afraid to "come out" right away. You set an example as an honest, respectable member of the community. You show through word and example that there is nothing to hide, no reason to duck your head and feel ashamed. In living this life, you become an ideal role model for your children.

Why doesn't Mommy/Daddy live with us? Why are you getting a divorce?

When answering this type of question, it is vital to make the point that the child is in no way responsible for the absence of a parent or the break-up of a marriage. Even if the marriage dissolved as the result of a difficult or sick child, it was the inability of one or both parents to cope that created the problem and led to the break up. It was not the fault of the child.

As pagans, we don't hold the belief that a relationship must last until " do us part." Traditional handfastings (at least the first one) are for one year and one day. Then the couple may decide whether to extend the relationship or say a friendly farewell.

Some pagans do not even practice a monogamous lifestyle. Even if those involved are polyamorous, the breakup of any relationship can be very difficult. Whether a parent has one or more lovers, children will bond both to their own parents and also to any other consistent adult in the family. When that person is gone from the relationship, the children may effectively lose a parental figure.

While most of us do hope that a relationship, particularly one with children, will last forever, sometimes it is just not realistic. People grow and change. Ideally, the couple spent enough time together to be certain of the match before entering into a legal marriage contract.

Whatever the reasons, it is our responsibility as pagans to be respectful of our relationships while we are in them, and to be honorable about the other person when it is over.

We respect our children by telling them the truth, within reason and without bashing the other parent. Children do not need to know the gory details, if there are any. They do have a right to know the generalities and whether or not the separation may be temporary or is definitely permanent. They have the right to expect a discussion as to the whereabouts of an absent parent and why they can only see a parent at certain times.

Why are we pagan? How do I explain our religion/ spirituality to my friends?

This differs from the next two "why can't I ..." questions in that it is often asked by children who were most likely not raised pagan from infancy and are trying to understand it. They want to be able to share with friends but are not sure how to go about that without risk. This child is probably comfortable with the family's chosen path.

There is another side to this question. Those raised pagan and surrounded by a pagan family and/or community may not be aware that paganism is not the path of the majority. They may not be aware that everyone doesn't feel and believe the same things.

The first question here is highly individual. Any answers are very personal and will vary according to the person. I can only say to be honest and speak from your heart. If you have explored other paths, let your child know. Be open to his or her own potential need for exploration as well. Telling them your truth, from the heart, will say more than all the books in the world possibly could.

While explaining why you have chosen a particular path, be wary of belittling other religions. Certainly there are pros and cons to all religions. All followers of a religion are not the same. There are misguided and destructive followers of paganism just as there are fearful, hateful followers of any religion. In following a spirituality or religion that we feel is "better," we do not serve that energy or those spirits by denigrating the paths of others.

As for explaining the family path to friends, I strongly recommend some creative, flexible thought before deciding on a strategy. How you go about doing this will largely depend on the individual you want to share this with. I have had some friends who were so open-minded that we quickly and easily progressed from the more acceptable New Age topics. On the other hand, I lost some good friends in middle school and high school as a result of being too open too quickly.

These days, paganism is much more accepted and is quickly moving into the mainstream. Some pagan families invite their children's friends to holiday rituals and pagan gatherings. While they never hide who they are, they are not always completely open about their religion initially or at school. There is a difference between being in-your-face blatant and simply being who you are. The former often indicates a need for attention.

Unfortunately, not everyone is accepting of other paths. While the children may have no issue with a pagan friend, their parents may be another story. A young friend of ours found a wonderful boyfriend when she went away to college. She has always been very open about her religion. They had planned to share a house off-campus when his parents found out that she is pagan. They threatened to take away his car and his college tuition if he continued seeing her. Sadly, this situation is a real possibility for pagan children, even today.

As pagan parents, we must decide how we want this issue handled. I have devoted chapter 10 entirely to the question of honesty versus secrecy. We need to decide how "out" we are willing to be in our communities before getting our children involved in our religion or spirituality. There may come a time when we are not ready to be open but our children refuse to keep it a secret.

Can you/I cast a spell on someone for love/revenge/good grades...?

I would hope that as a parent, the answer to this would be very clearly "No." This is another case of *can* versus *should*. Followers of Earth-based religions do not interfere in the free will of another. We do not send out destructive or controlling energy because we know it will return to us.

However, it is not always an easy task to explain this to a child who feels invincible and knows with the melodrama of youth that they will certainly die if they do not get what they feel so strongly about. This is one reason why we must stress balance and responsibility when raising children in spiritual-magical paths. While it is true that magic is really just about creating change in one's reality, we don't use ritual magic or spells as an excuse for growth or as something to hide behind.

As pagans, we understand that we receive the same type of energy we put out. This extends from spell work to thoughts and from gossip to actions. Therefore, if you would not want someone else to include you in such a spell, don't do it. This should carry over to all our actions. Treat others as you would be treated is pretty good advice, no matter where it comes from.

The other major reason to avoid these kinds of spells is the end result. Not only may they backfire, but you need to be very skilled, very clear, and very specific before engaging in any form of magic. You may get what you ask for and find it is either not specifically what you really wanted or it is not what you expected.

Ask a child who is interested in a love spell how she would feel if she were magically bound to someone who turned out to be a very self-centered or nasty person. An individual generally feels the need for a love spell for two reasons. Either she desires a person who is clearly not interested or she is afraid to get to know the person and ask him or her out. In the first case, it is best to move on and find someone who is interested while working on any personal esteem issues that may be contributing. In the second case, you need to handle your fear first and work within this reality. You might ask the love interest out for ice cream or just start a conversation and see where it goes. This is real life, and magic should not be used to try to avoid it.

As far as a spell for good grades goes, it would be most beneficial to cast one on yourself. I used several techniques when in school for learning and grades. On occasion, I would telepathically receive the answer from a spirit guide or even the teacher. However, we accomplish nothing if our grades are not our own. We need to learn and retain this information or abilities for future success. What worked best for me from grammar school through graduate school were spells and other techniques to improve my own memory and access to stored information, concentration, ability to quickly and easily absorb and process what I was learning; anything that helped me learn and remember better.

Am I a witch/druid/shaman/etc.?

The answer to this will very likely depend on your point of view as to who is and who is not any of these things. For some people, you are automatically a witch if your family follows that path or you have decided that you are. However, many paths require a period of training or other criteria to attain the title of Druid or Shaman or Vitki.

For example in the Order of Bards, Ovates, and Druids (OBOD), we all follow a druidic path and certainly consider ourselves druids. Within OBOD tradition, we are not all Druids, meaning we have not all completed the necessary training for admittance into the Druid Grade. In a seed-group we were part of for a number of years, we called our children Baby Bards. At that time, many of them were not even old enough to speak yet, let alone "Bard out." Our children are children and, until they choose to follow the druidic path, they are not druids.

This chapter will certainly not answer all of your family's tough questions. It is a good overview of some of the more common ones. While my answers may not be right for your family, it is my hope that they will give you a place to begin when deciding what to say. Often we need to get clear on our own beliefs and feelings first. After that, the answers that are right for us seem to flow easily.

As parents, we need to avoid the temptation or expectation that we will be perfect and all-knowing individuals. We are who and what we are, and having children does not often change that significantly. What we can do is to strive toward being the best individuals and role models we can. We can admit that we are human and are still learning. Most importantly, we can always be there with unconditional love and support for our children.

Chapter 9
Spirituality

I separate spirituality and religion in this book. While both are interrelated, this separation makes things easier to discuss in a book and it allows me to show clearly that one may follow a spiritual path without belonging to a religion. Spirituality, as far as this book is concerned, is that innate sense of one's connection to All of Life. On the other hand, religion in this book includes religious rituals and beliefs.

Many pagans find that they do not fit within any of the self-described religions although they may be intensely spiritual. We enter this reality as purely spiritual beings, working to integrate our spiritual energies into a purely physical realm. Very young children remain spiritual beings unless their families or societies give them reason to block this experience. The young are naturally spiritual and tend toward being respectful.

The total household atmosphere and the everyday activities of family members are the main influences that foster a child's innate spirituality. If the family is respectful toward other people and the natural world, it is likely that the child will behave in similar ways. Of course, other relationships will affect any child's behavior. Children emulate those they trust and respect. They also tend to conform to varying degrees to fit in with peers.

Pagan parents try to foster respectful spiritual values at home. We pray over meals, particularly when eating meat. We hold to the eight holidays and will often honor the full or new moon phases. We include our children in appropriate rituals and encourage their participation when they show an interest.

In our family, we thank the garden spirits and spirits of this place when we work in our garden or pick native herbs. Karl learns about human interactions with and perceptions of animals from the wildlife rehabilitation organization that we work with. He is well aware that our educational birds can no longer fly free, mainly because of interactions with humans, and he knows the signs of poisoning all too well.

To many pagans, spirituality is about those innate and intuitive connections with the natural world. Even those pagans who have never slept under the stars in the wilderness feel their connections with "All Our Relations." It is important that these feelings and experiences become more than mental exercises to be honored indoors at the appropriate holidays.

Connecting with Nature

You might try to get outside with your family whenever possible. This can be enormously beneficial on a physical and psychological level. With a goal of connecting to the spirits of the land, it can become a truly magical experience. Even if you can only get to an outdoor playground or find a tree on a city street, the spirits of nature are there. They may be sleeping, waiting for a pagan to wake them from their protective sleep, but they are there. It is within our power to create sacred sites, even if only for ourselves.

I was fortunate to have grown up on several wooded acres completely surrounded by a state forest and game preserve. There was a sacred valley, filled with power and spirits, that accepted me as one of its own. I would retreat to this place for comfort and guidance. It was where I headed when I was upset or overwhelmed. To this day, I return to that valley on a psychic level for peace and guidance.

However, I have not always been so fortunate as to live in a wilderness area. Nor have I always had the time or means to be able to travel to a state or national park. Even in the absence of an obvious wilderness, the spirits of the wild have found me. In two of our apartments, we had one tree outside one window. These trees became my daily lifeline to the natural world.

In Connecticut, we found a small city park, filled with beer bottles and old condoms. After some time spent meditating and sending out energy blessings, this park came alive with spirit energy. We even began to see evidence of wild animal activity as the squirrels, deer, and birds moved back in.

Even when I was locked in a laboratory, sometimes for more than twelve hours per day, my office plants helped me to center and balance. At least once each day, I would sit and silently meditate on the plants. The chemists working for me called it my "veg out" time. This time, spent communing with the spirits and filling myself and my work space with sacred energy, worked wonders for my well-being as well as my productivity and my ability to be a good scientist and manager.

In the city, although we have access to wilderness areas, we know all the trees on the street. The sagebrush and ricegrass on the highway where we walk our dog are our friends. We need only to tune in and the spirit world awakens from its hibernation, eager to interact with those who would acknowledge and honor its existence.

Children respond well to attuning to Nature spirits. The following exercise is designed specifically to connect with the spirits of the natural world. Use this to practice attuning to trees, metals, stones, crystals, lakes, etc. Vary it as you choose to include all kinds of different experiences, including things we may not view as natural, like bicycles and computers.

Nature Spirit Attunement Exercise

Begin by having the children feel and inspect whatever it is they will be "entering" during the meditation. Then have them get comfortable either sitting or lying down. If possible, have them hold the objects during meditation.

Count them down from ten to one or guide them to enter a light trance in your usual way.

Guide them to see the objects before them, big as a house or bigger. Have them inspect the outside of the objects. Teach them to be respectful by asking permission to enter the objects. Tell them to trust whatever comes up. If permission is denied, try another object or wait until the child is better prepared. It may be beneficial to guide one child at a time, reporting the experience as it occurs. You can either record this with a tape recorder or write it down so details are not lost. This is also a great way for children to develop their own abilities to retain information obtained in Other realties.

If permission is granted, guide them to enter the objects through a door in the side of the object. Ask them what they see inside. Ask what the temperature is, the light level, how the walls feel. Ask if there are any sounds or smells. Get all of their senses involved in the experience.

Next, have them explore the object. Ask if they encounter any beings within the object.

When they have explored most of the object or seem ready to come out, guide them back to the door they entered. Have them stop before leaving and give thanks to any *one* or any *thing* they encountered. Instruct them to ask if there are any last messages before they return to everyday reality. Give them some time to receive these.

Guide them back out through the door. As they leave, have them stop at the door, take a last look at the object, and leave an offering of thanks to the spirit of the object for this experience.

Count them back up from one to ten as usual or in the same format you counted them down.

This respect and gratitude is an important facet of pagan spirituality. The more respectful we are, the more teaching and support we will receive from the Other Worlds. Our greatest power flows through us from the Universe. It does not belong to us, and it cannot be depleted as long as we are in alignment with Spirit.

When we interact with the spirits, Gods, and Goddesses, we enter into a give-and-take relationship with them. We do not deny our own innate divinity and become the servants of these beings; neither do we expect them to become our slaves. We make offerings and give prayers and rituals of thanks to honor the gifts we receive on a daily basis. In this way, we continue the energetic cycle of blessings and beneficial energy.

This is a similar concept to that of treating other physical beings as we would be treated. We would not, under normal conditions, continue to assist and give to a person who offered us no thanks or respect back, particularly if that person was abusive. We should not expect the spirits to continue to give selflessly. Even if they would do so, we would dishonor both them and ourselves by living this kind of life.

I mentioned the prayer we offer during meals in an earlier chapter. This may remind you of the Christian grace, but its meanings and origins are much deeper and more ancient than that. In honoring these beings with a prayer before eating, we create each meal as a ceremonial meal. We release any unwanted energies from our food and imbue it with blessed and sacred energies.

Indigenous peoples honored the spirits of the animals they needed to kill for food and other essential items. They respected the fact that these "relations" filled a vital place for us in the cycle of life. These animals were our brothers and sisters as well as our teachers and guides. We all shared the need for food and sustenance in the planetary life cycle. It was understood and accepted that we may also become a meal for one of them someday. Even if we did not, our ashes would become one with the ashes of all our relations and continue to create life on this planet.

In modern society, many people have adopted the belief that animals are lower forms of life deserving of little to no respect. Many people feel that animals were put on this Earth for us to use and discard as we choose. They are not sentient beings; they are commodities.

This is not a common pagan belief. The majority of pagans will at least offer lip-service to an opposing viewpoint. I have had many teachers who were in animal form, both in this reality and in Others. I have been told by some of my animal allies that they are aspects of me and that we are One. Many of you have had these same feelings or experiences.

Whether we view these beings as potential species for our own reincarnation as the manifestations of our spirit guides or simply as other children of Mother Earth, they deserve our respect. Those who walk their Earth journey with respect for All of Life will receive respect and power from the natural world. The only way our children will grow up in this way is if we hold that energy within the family and act accordingly.

It is this respect for other beings, no matter what species—including the tree and stone people—that leads to respect and honor among our own species. I believe a lack of connection with our world and respect for Self and others to be at the center of most of the crime issues in modern society.

Wild Plant Walks

Periodically, I take our son on herb walks to replenish our smudge and medicine supplies. This is a great way to introduce the concept of give and take with young children. It is also a wonderful method for teaching the basics of plant identification and to foster a connection with the land.

Below, I describe a sagebrush-picking expedition. This is an example that can be greatly varied, depending on your needs at the time. You may choose to go on identification walks with your children first. This way they can get an idea of what the plants are and the environment in which they live. Play amateur naturalist with your children as you both learn about the plants, animals, geology, and water cycles in your area.

There is one strong caution I would give any parents who may be considering taking children on medicinal or edible plant walks. Do not allow a child to put anything in his or her mouth until both of you are absolutely certain what it is. It is a very good idea to educate yourself on the poisonous plants in your area and learn how to identify them. Then teach your children which ones to avoid. A good rule of thumb is: if in doubt, don't touch it.

Unless you are an expert at mushroom identification, never taste or eat a wild mushroom and caution your children about the dangers of this. Mushrooms contain an incredibly large number of complex chemical compounds. Many of these are harmless, some are hallucinogenic, and many are dangerously toxic.

If you are picking plants that you plan to ingest in any form, it is also advisable to avoid areas that are close to highways. The plants near roadways will absorb any petroleum products that leak onto the ground as well as the airborne exhaust of passing vehicles.

Many species of edible or medicinal plant life bear strong similarities to poisonous species. Ingestion of many of these other species can be debilitating, even fatal. Unless you really know your identification well, I would recommend avoiding any of the similar species in the wild. I made it a point not to put any wild plant in my mouth around our son until he was old enough to understand that some plants can hurt him—and old enough to know that that is not the time to argue with a "No."

Now he is old enough to understand these things without being told. From our walks, he can pick out nearly all of the local native plants and quite a few from other habitats. He also knows that we do not remove parts of plants for fun or on a whim. A sagebrush-picking trip is a serious (although fun) event.

Picking Sagebrush

We begin by choosing a place where we have not picked recently. It is important to recognize the potential effects of over-harvesting one area. We let the other places "rest" for a while. We gather up our water bottle, a paper bag for collection, and any offerings we may want to leave in return for our sagebrush.

A paper bag is preferable to a plastic bag for drying plants although it doesn't really matter what you collect them in. Plastic bags retain the moisture of plants, preventing drying and increasing the possibility of mold growth. You may also wish to hang plants to dry. In the desert Southwest, water is about as valuable as gold in most areas. Many times we feel that this is the best offering we can give to the plants, and we usually carry an extra water bottle. Other offerings may be sacred herbs, corn, a crystal, or simply a blessing and sending of loving energy.

Once we get to the area we are going to harvest, we take some time to be quiet and center our energies. We ask permission from the Spirits of Place and wait for an answer. If we get an uneasy or doubtful feeling, we try another spot or go home. We find the oldest bush in the area and leave our offering. This may be a bush that is obviously larger and older, but it may be just a feeling that we have. Then we each take a small piece of sagebrush and put it in our mouths. As we chew on the sagebrush, we go wherever we are led for harvesting.

We pick only as much as we need, being sure not to take too much from one bush. Then we move on until we either feel a clear signal that we have taken enough or we have the amount we believe is enough. We leave an offering at each bush we harvest from along with a prayer of thanks.

When we are finished, we return to the oldest bush and give thanks for the gifts of this sagebrush. We promise to use it in a sacred manner and always to honor the spirits of the land. Then we come home and keep our promises.

Purification

Some form of purification and cleansing is part of most spiritual paths. We may purify ourselves, our homes, sacred space of Circles or other ritual space, or just about anything we wish to be free of unwanted energies and beings. Two methods of purification are easy for children to learn and participate in.

The smudge ceremony is something that even a toddler can assist with. Children should always be supervised around matches and anything that is burning. However, this is a simple yet profound ritual that really evokes a sense of reverence and gratitude. It is a ritual and as such could easily have been included in the following chapter.

I include it here for two reasons. One reason is its innate spiritual feel. Many people feel it is more of a moving meditation than a true ritual although for some it is akin to casting a Circle and calling directions. With conditioning, the lighting of the smudge alone can be a trance-induction method. Rather than being a full ritual in itself, it is frequently a form of ritual preparation.

The other reason is that it is a borrowed element of Native cultures. Most world cultures have some form of purification or consecration by fire, often burning herbs. But the sagebrush-cedar-sweetgrass-copal smudge ceremony is typically indigenous to the Americas, even though many scholars believe it is a recent development. Most neo-pagans do not follow traditional, indigenous "American" religions although many of us incorporate some of their spiritual elements into our own paths. Therefore, while it may be included within some neo-pagan spiritual paths, it is not really part of most of these religions.

With a basic understanding of the ceremony, it is a simple thing to come up with ways for children to participate. Our son began when he was a little over one year old. Although he could stand, he was a bit unsteady on his feet, so he sat and held his arms out (just like Mommy and Daddy) while we wafted the smoke around him. As he showed more interest, I often carried him with me when I smudged our home.

By two years old, he actively participated in any way he could. Only a year later, he was allowed to carry a smudge stick around the house with supervision and had created his own smudge fan. Now he often decides when something or someone needs smudging and is perfectly capable of performing the ceremony on his own.

Feel free to experiment with the smudge and drum purification ceremonies that follow to discover what works best for you and your family. Older children can take a more active role. When I was approximately five years old, I was allowed to carry the incense or smudge for my mother. Eventually, I was old enough to light it with supervision. And by the time I reached junior high school, I could burn candles and incense alone in my room.

The Smudge Ceremony

You will need: A source of purifying smoke, such as smudge sticks or loose herbs such as sagebrush (*Artemisia* spp.), sweetgrass, or incenses such as sandalwood and myrrh; matches or a lighter; a candle   is recommended for a continuing flame, especially for smudge sticks, which may be difficult to maintain smoking; a heat-resistant container or incense burner;   Optional - a feather or fan.

Take a moment to center yourself. It may help to count yourself down from ten to one, remembering to breathe deeply and from the diaphragm.

Light your smudge with respect. Invite the smoke of the sacred herbs to purify your energy and this space.

Using your feather or fan to move the smoke or carrying the smudge stick with you, offer the sacred smoke to the six directions: North, East, South, West, Earth, and Sky; and to the Great Spirit in the center, which permeates all things. Offer blessings of respect and gratitude to each of these.

Beginning at the navel, bathe yourself in the sacred and purifying smoke. Move the smoke up to your heart area, then over your head, along your back, down to your feet, and back up to your navel.

As the smoke moves along your body, feel yourself center deeply. Breathe deeply of the smoke. See your worries and tensions dissolve in the warmth as they are carried up and away by the smoke. Ask the smoke of the sacred herbs once again to purify your energy, to clear you of all limitations, and to help you become a clear and protected channel for healing energy.

Offer the smoke once more to each of the six directions and the Creator. Give thanks to them for their presence in your life. Thank the smoke of these sacred herbs for their assistance in purifying your energy.

*Some individuals and groups believe that once a smudge is burning, it should be left to burn itself out. The truth of this will depend on your beliefs and experience. In my experience, allowing something to burn for extended periods of time is not always possible or preferable. In my journeying and work with these sacred plants, I have been taught that whether I extinguish the flame or leave it to burn itself out is not important, provided my every action is made in respect and honor.

The other purification method that gets children actively involved is the drum purification ceremony. Children tend to find this one lots of fun. While this assists them in maintaining an interest, as a parent or guide it is important that they do not get carried away with the fun and lose the spiritual connection and sense of reverence. They can follow your lead with a rattle, a bell, small drum, or even clapping their hands. It is the attitude and energy we create that is most important. Therefore, a home-made film canister rattle or a touristy rubber and cardboard drum will do just fine.

Drum Purification Ceremony

Take several deep breaths and center yourself. Begin to beat the drum. In determining the speed of the beat, go with what feels right to you at the time. It is generally recommended that this be faster than a heartbeat.

Continue to beat the drum until you feel yourself center deeply and enter the trance state.

Holding the drum up and out from your body, offer its sound to each of the four directions. Then offer it to the Sky and the Earth. Then to the center again, to offer it to the Creator.

Continue to drum at the pace that resonates best for you along your entire body, stopping at each chakra for a few moments. Allow the sound and energy of the drum to harmonize your energy systems and clear unwanted vibrations. Hold the drum at each chakra or any area that feels the need, drumming until you feel this area come into balance with the rest of your system.

Hold the drum out to center once more as an offering of thanks to the Creator. Beat four times more quickly and then end with one strong beat.

When I think of spirituality, the main thing that comes to mind is the web that connects us with All of Life. This includes spirit beings and those life forms that modern science may or may not recognize as being sentient, or even alive. Within this type of belief system, every action becomes sacred, or should. We recognize that everything we choose to do reflects our spirituality and our deepest Selves. Our spirituality is inherent in our treatment of other people and the natural world. This is something that we want to pass on to our children. Certainly we do so by example through how we live our lives.

Elemental Attunement

As children explore and become more connected to this world, they naturally fall in love with the Earth and all Her creatures. How many of us could not (or still cannot) resist a mud puddle, a flower, or a beautiful rock? I first began my rock collection when I was seven years old, and it continues to grow today. In modern society, the key seems to be keeping our children in love with the Earth and encouraging their natural respect for all things.

One way to do this is to teach kids the various ways to attune to the Earth. For children, this is usually quite natural. Physical activities and games are often the best way for children to stay in tune. Due to their attention and energy levels, depending on the age of the child, it's best to keep the meditations and passive visualizations to a minimum. Once we are connected on a spiritual and physical level, respect follows naturally. [i]

Association Webs

For each element, creating an association web can be a fun method to discover additional ways to encourage your children's connection with Nature. It can be a written exercise or played as a game with as many players as you choose.

The main goal is to give the children one word, in this case, an element. They are then responsible for writing or calling out anything that comes to mind when they hear the name of the element. If they cannot write yet, you may want to record their answers. With more than one player, answers will spark new associations in each of the players' minds and may create some interesting (and long-lived) games.

You may want to pay attention to any unusual answers or anything that is related to past events.

These are often keys to deeper meanings or possibly difficult situations that the child may be ready to deal with. In any event, most of the associations they come up with will give you ideas of new games or exercises that will deepen their awareness of the elements and increase their abilities to work with each element.

Earth

Attuning to the Earth by growing things is a fun and educational method for teaching children about any number of things, from physical science to interactions with fairies and plant devas. Not only does this allow them to get our hands dirty and witness the miracle of life, but through growing things they recognize the cycles of life and learn to be stewards of the Earth. This is a great process for children. They get a real sense of accomplishment and confidence in caring for "their" plants.

Every child who can understand simple directions can grow a small plant from a bean. Most of us did this in elementary school. Keep the bean moist in a wet paper towel or sponge until it sprouts. Once the sprout begins to grow, plant it in some potting soil. Make sure it gets sun and water, and it will be just fine.

You may also want to teach children to grow plants from seed. This generally takes no longer than sprouting beans and, depending on the seed, your child can produce a flower or vegetable for additional wonder. When space was an issue and we had no yard of our own, I grew tomatoes and peppers in big containers. While they did not get as big as store-bought vegetables, it was wonderful to have ones we grew and loved. Strawberry and blueberry plants are also easy to grow indoors and delight everyone.

If you do have the space, give your children a corner of your garden or yard for their own gardens. Our son thoroughly enjoys helping me plant and water his garden. The first year, he was just two years old and we planted sunflowers, cantaloupes, chile peppers, and peas. He was amazed by the entire process and learned some patience along the way. During his anti-vegetable period, he would even eat the peas out of the pod, just because they were his peas and the pods were so cool!

Depending on the age of the child, blessings and rituals for the planting and harvesting of the garden add to the sacredness and respect that children gain from the experience. Be sure to give thanks for each flower and all the food that you receive from the Earth. Explain the interconnections involved in life on Earth and how none of us exist independent of other life.

Very young children have an innate connection to life and energy. Even a child who is not yet walking will be attracted to the sight of a parent holding out open hands over a seedling and speaking simple blessings. Most children will instinctively mimic this act. As your children's language and comprehension skills advance, they will most likely want to speak the blessings themselves.

Older children, particularly those that were not raised in this way from birth, may feel silly or uncomfortable doing this. It is best not to pressure them to do so. Merely continue as you normally would, neither hiding your actions nor expecting the child to participate. When they are ready to participate, they will, although they may begin to do so in secret. And if they do not, we allow them their freedom to choose.

Rocks

Now what about those rock collections? I still have one. I'll bet many of you do, too. Mine has grown from a general collection of simple igneous, metamorphic, and sedimentary stones to a widely varied tool kit of crystals and stones for all types of self-development and healing. Our son's collection rivals mine already.

175

Rocks are a great way to connect, not only with the Earth element, but also with Other Worlds. Many rocks serve as gateways to other realities, as well as storing ancient wisdom and memories. If your child has an interest in rocks, I would suggest encouraging that. The Nature Spirit Attunement Exercise in this chapter is an excellent way to connect with the spirits of the stones and access the wisdom stored within each.

Air

Air can be an elusive element unless a weather system is present that creates wind. It is also one element that may require related objects for a child to work well with. Until children are comfortable with abstract or philosophical ideas (sometimes not until they are teens), they may need to focus more on the effects of air and wind or on the animals and things that rely on air or wind.

For the baby and toddler, dandelion fuzz can be the tool for their very first natural magic. Dandelions grow in almost all areas and most of us are familiar with making wishes while blowing the fuzz from them at the end of their season. This is very similar to the wish-spells associated with blowing out birthday candles. Just as in any form of magic, belief and emotion are vital to the success of a dandelion fuzz wish. With very young children, a parent may need to provide this initially.

Dandelion Fuzz Wishes

Before going outside to find a dandelion in fuzz, decide on the wish you will be asking for. Then go outside with that wish in your minds and ask to be led to the dandelion that wants to help you make this wish come true.

Ask before picking the dandelion of your choice. When permission is given, pick it with a prayer of thanks. If your child is able, have him or her say thank you along with you as you pick the plant.

Hold the dandelion between you and have the child hold it gently with you. Older children can hold the plant on their own. Repeat the wish out loud. If they are old enough, have them imagine the wish growing really big. Older children should be encouraged to use all their senses to make the wish very real. Then blow the wish out into the dandelion fuzz and watch as it is carried off into the air.

Tell them that the wish is now part of the fuzz and that the air will carry it to the Great Spirit or God and Goddess.

Older children may prefer to work with weather. Children over the age of ten may perceive the game of Dandelion Fuzz Wishes as being childish. Honoring and attuning to wind-driven weather systems is a powerful way of aligning with the element of Air as well as increasing a feeling of interconnection and respect for Nature. This exercise is also one way to redirect the focus of any child who may be afraid of storms.

Become the Storm

This exercise can easily be altered to assist you with becoming a bird or a kite or anything else you choose.

As soon as the wind begins to pick up and, as long as it is safe, sit with your children by a window and watch the wind move in. Guide everyone to take a deep breath and feel the wind. If possible, you may prefer to open the window a bit to help your children feel it.

Thank the wind and the weather for their presence and for the benefits they bring. Ask that they share their essence with you and speak to your Spirits.

Guide your children to continue taking deep breaths and to imagine becoming the wind and its power. Encourage them to include all five of their physical senses as they become the storm. Suggest that they listen to the voice of the storm and hear anything it may say to them.

Maintain this as long as you wish or until your children begin to come back to their bodies and get fidgety. Bring them back slowly and gently by guiding them to feel their bodies, the chairs they are sitting on, the temperature of the room, etc.

Discuss your experiences or record them in your personal journals.

Air can be also seen as the breath, or the kiss, of the Great Spirit. Children can easily visualize being kissed or touched by this Divinity each time they feel even a slight breeze. Teaching this to children can remind them, as they go about their everyday activities, that they are safe and loved by the Gods. The breathing exercises in chapter 3 are also highly recommended for connecting to the power and influence of Air as Breath.

Fire

Most of us attune to Fire instinctively in the summer. Temperatures are warmer, we lie out in the sun, and we may become more physically active. Summer is often a child's favorite time of year. And the Sun is the best way to work with Fire for young children.

Using the Becoming the Storm exercise given above, anyone can become the sun or a bonfire or a candle flame with a few alterations to the specifics of the exercise. This is an ideal exercise to do anytime you are spending some quiet time outside in the sunshine. It is perfect for anyone "laying out" to get a suntan, as is the next exercise.

Your Inner Sun

Count your children down from ten to one, reminding them periodically to take deep breaths.

Guide them to see a golden star, or a small sun, in the center of their bodies. Describe it in great detail, using imagery that will involve as many of their senses as possible.

Guide them to see and feel this golden star in their centers expand and glow brightly. Its radiance extends out beyond their bodies in a protective egg of light.

Suggest to them that this inner sun will keep them safe and healthy and that they can use it in any way they choose. Tell them that whenever they need help making decisions, all they need to do is look to their inner suns. It will give them all the answers they need by glowing brighter or dimmer.

Give them some time to experience this inner sun fully before counting them back up from one to ten.

Discuss the experience or allow them to write it in their personal journals.

Water

Water is another easy element for a child to attune to. Working with it can often be combined with Earth attunement exercises. For example, when you water your house plants or garden, thank the water and charge it with beneficial energies. The Become the Storm exercise is also excellent to use during rainstorms, to attune to the water as well as the wind in a storm. The Nature Spirit Attunement exercise is recommended for attuning to the spirits of lakes, rivers, or any body of water, even a house fountain.

For children, water attunement serves another very important purpose. It helps them to connect with emotion. In many modern societies, emotion is something to be hidden from all but our closest friends. An understanding of one's feelings and the ability to experience them is often seen as a weakness, rather than as the strength it really is. Unfortunately, this belief is particularly ingrained into our young boys.

Emotion is one important aspect of the water element. As such, it should be given the respect and attention that it deserves. Pagan children benefit in many ways from working with this element and from the example of strong yet sensitive pagan men and women. Far too often in our society, people cannot even give a name to their feelings, let alone accept and honor them. This creates blocks in one's energy field and can contribute to soul fragmentation.

One simple way to teach self-knowledge is scrying. While many pagans use the scrying bowl or mirror for divination, it works in much the same way to put children in touch with their emotions and inner selves. A bowl, preferably black, filled with water serves as a focal point. This allows you to be objective in what you see, releasing the analytical mind that would normally interfere with these matters.

Scrying for Self-Knowledge

Set aside a bowl to be used only for this purpose. It is preferable for each family member to have his or her own bowl for scrying. It is preferred that the interior of the bowl be black or have no decorations, but this is not necessary.

Even young children can be taught to scry. The amount of guidance they require will depend on the disposition and age of the individual child. If you are working with young children, under the age of five, guide them through the exercise below, periodically stopping to ask them what they feel or see.

Fill the bowl at least halfway with water. Pass first your left hand, then your right hand over the surface of the water, aligning your energy with that of the water. Ask that the spirit of the water allow you to see your Self honestly and gently in the bowl. If there is a certain situation or emotion you need to deal with, ask for specific guidance in seeing this clearly.

Give yourself time to see whatever shows up. If you see only symbols, ask that they be made clearer or give yourself additional time to allow the meanings to flow into your conscious mind. Know that you can focus on specific elements of the image by simply relaxing and allowing yourself to become more open. What you are looking at in this exercise is your own inner Self, and you control your access to it.

Keep in mind that you may not "see" anything. Be aware of any thoughts, feelings, or memories that come to mind. Allow them to pass you by so your mind does not wander, but if the same ones keep coming up, give them your attention to determine if they are bringing you a message.

If you need guidance in making a decision or handling something differently in the future, ask for it. Your spirit guides and the spirit of the water will hear you.

Ask if there is anything else you need to see at this time and give yourself time to experience whatever may come up.

When you are satisfied that the greatest benefit was achieved in this session, give thanks to the spirit of the water and to your Self. Dispose of the water with respect and thanks, either in a garden or as an offering to the spirits of your home.

Earth Stewardship

Since most pagans are followers of Earth-based or Goddess-based religions, Earth stewardship can be a vital expression of their spirituality. For some this is achieved simply, through honoring the spirits of the land in prayer and meditation. Others feel they are called to get more actively involved through alternative lifestyle choices, career choices, or involvement with activist organizations.

Most pagan parents tend to support these choices if their children feel drawn to them. It certainly benefits your children if you are also involved with caring for the Earth in some way. The health and survival of humans and many other species depends on our ability to live in harmony and attunement with our world. We desperately need to develop less harmful power sources and more constructive ways of dealing with our global and individual differences.

But just as importantly, these are also lifestyle choices that will allow our children to incorporate their spirituality with other aspects of their lives. While this is possible in almost any situation, some lifestyle choices are inherently more spiritual and healthy than others. If a child feels drawn to a choice that allows a concrete means of honoring the Earth and the God and Goddess, they deserve all the support we can give them.

One of the best goals we can hope to achieve as pagan parents is to teach our children that every action—our every thought—has power. Therefore, it is vital that we live our lives as though each act is a spiritual and sacred one. When we call upon the Spirits of the directions, our spirit guides, or the Gods, we pray "May our every action honor You." In this way, spirituality is not some separate aspect of life to be solely encased within a religious framework. It becomes life itself, and we learn to walk each day as the spiritual beings that we are.

i.   the preceding two paragraphs and much of this section on growing things were first

      published in an article entitled, "Attuning to Earth," in the Summer 1998 issue of

      Circle Network News.

Chapter 10
Religion

Religion is generally defined as the belief in and worship of a Deity or Deities. It also includes the faith, beliefs, and system of worship or service to those Deities. As I said before, religion and spirituality are not necessarily mutually exclusive. I separate them for reasons of clarity and order in this book, as well as for those reasons described in the previous chapter.

The pagan relationship to the Gods and Goddesses is a complex one that varies not only with the individual but also with the path or tradition. Although children may be raised in one path, they may feel a strong connection or attraction to Deities of other pantheons. This is generally accepted in pagan homes, no matter which path the family follows.

Differing Beliefs

The main exception that can also cause some concern is when pagan children develop an interest in the God and religion of the monotheistic religions. This may cause some discomfort and upset in a pagan family.

The divisive issues between pagans and Christians are well known. There is no real point in discussing this issue here, except as it relates to the raising of children within a pagan tradition. This is another situation where we as parents must examine our own reactions if a child decides that he or she is a Christian. Before discriminating or forbidding it, ask yourself why you are reacting in this way. Does your behavior benefit your child and will it prevent this interest? Are you adopting the same kind of belief and attitude that leads Christians to become missionaries? How would you (or did you) feel if a parent refused to allow your pagan interest?

Many families will allow their children to explore Christianity (or any other religion) while insisting that they respect the traditions of their family. This is often accompanied by the family's willingness to respect the child's preferences. Some families will even encourage this exploration of other paths, including Christianity.

Although some children may continue to be drawn to the mystical side of the monotheistic religions, it does appear that few pagan children continue along this type of path for long. The vast majority of children who were raised pagan are not willing to accept a belief system that denigrates all others and would sentence their families to eternal damnation merely for holding differing beliefs. Once they have gained an experiential understanding of the limitations and intolerance of such a path, they generally move on in their search.

Through supporting, or at least allowing, their search, we demonstrate our unconditional love for our children. We also reduce the risk that they will resent us for impeding an honest spiritual interest. We do not want to become those intolerant people we warn our children about.

There is another benefit to allowing this search. If a child is becoming involved with a different religion out of rebellion or revenge, you can eliminate the desired effects of this behavior and may effectively defuse the situation. When you forbid or punish in situations like this, there is a good chance that you will only drive your children further away.

With that said, let's turn our attention to the various aspects of raising children within the pagan religions. As pagans, what are the most obvious aspects of our religions? Certainly, our rituals are the most obvious. These are also the most complex, and we will discuss these in a later chapter. But there are other ways that we work with and honor the Deities and spirits that are an integral part of any pagan's life. These generally include altars and the various spiritual and magical tools we use.

Altars

All pagans have some form of altar, whether it is a talisman hung innocently on a doorknob, a few crystals on a shelf, or a separate altar room. Altars may take the form of a few well-chosen objects on a desk at work or they may be altars-in-a-box, hidden under living room tables. Whatever form they take, an altar is a focal point as well as a means of connecting with one's honored spirits.

The main goal of a family altar is to become an honoring place for that which is special to the individual or group. There are innumerable altars to Family in homes that may not recognize them as such. A piano or mantel with photos of family members is a form of altar. For a pagan family, we can create altars and assist our children in creating their own first altars by simply being creative and flexible.

Just as you were willing to recognize the possibility of Elmo as a spirit guide, you should remain open to your children's innate creativity and personal symbolism. A child's altar may be a special place for favorite rocks, a garden shrine, or a beloved tree. The altars of children are often much more freeform than that of an adult but, as they get older, they do tend to accumulate a lot of altar stuff.

While this is true for most pagans, we can be instrumental in teaching our children the value of more formal altars. In doing so, we can guide them in creating a special space for those energies they feel most attuned to and they want to bring into their lives. The best way to start is to work with your child and decide on a spot for the altar to be.

Give the child the choice of several places in your home or the child's room. It is important to know whether or not the child wants the altar to be private. If so, the inside of a closet or a hidden corner of a bedroom is probably the best choice. When I was a young teenager, my altar took up the middle shelf of a bookcase in my room. I kept a large cloth over the bookcase, hiding my from obvious view. Not only did this keep it safe from prying eyes, but it also preserved the special energy of that small space.

I would also suggest having a family discussion ahead of time regarding altars and the privacy and respect they are due. Without an agreement among the family that these altars are sacred and are not to be disturbed by siblings for any reason, then you are just setting your family up for fights and hurt feelings. If there are pets in the house, this should be kept in mind when planning the location of an altar. Dogs can easily knock over a floor altar, and a cat wanting food or attention at 3 A.M. may walk across a tabletop altar on purpose.

The next step is to sit down with your children and discuss their needs and desires. Do they want an altar cloth and if so, what color? Are there specific animals, rocks, or Deities that they feel connected to, and how can they best represent that in an age-appropriate way?

Toddlers may have difficulty with the language or even with analyzing spirituality in this way. It is most effective to go about this like a game. Children over the age of two can normally let you know where they want their special table set up. You may want to take them to a metaphysical shop or a fabric store and see if they are drawn to anything in particular. You can also do this at home by collecting their favorite things and deciding together what should be included.

Since children can be attracted to anything that catches their eyes at the time, you may want to ask specifically if they want those items for their altars. Pick each item up and carry it with you. When they are finished looking, show them all the things once more and determine which are really special enough to bring home.

For the older child, this discussion is probably unnecessary unless the entire family is very new to paganism. By the time children who have been raised pagan are six or seven, they are generally well aware of altars and their uses. For very young children, you may prefer to create small altars for them in the beginning.

Our son created his first formal altar when he was a little over three years old. Out of the blue, he decided that he wanted his very own altar in his room. We searched in the garage for something to use as a base and came up with Daddy's old small ironing board. Our son set it down just under his window. I showed him the remaining blue cloth from his holiday calendar and he decided that was perfect for him.

Then he ran all over the house collecting his rocks, statues, and candles. He decided that his baby tree should stay in the living room, but he wanted his little Earth flag on the side of the altar. He was so happy and proud of his altar that he told everyone that came to our house about it. Everyone had to go see it, even the non-pagans that I worked with at the time. They may not have understood it, but he was so ecstatic about it, they just had to be happy for him.

These days, he has several altars in his room that change over time. He has three formal altars that I am aware of, filled with statues, candles, stones, medicine pouches, plants, and more. On his bedposts, he keeps special pendants and amulets along with herb bags.

While we may not understand the placement of certain items, children tend to take this very seriously. Each of these items has a special and specific place. Sometimes these are for practical reasons. For example, a stuffed dragon or special amulet needs to be in reach during the night, just in case. Other times, it is purely Spirit that guides them. To allow their altars to take the form the child needs them to is empowering for the children.

Another form of a bedside altar may involve stuffed animals or dolls. Bedtime is frequently when children need to feel the safest. Stuffed animals and dolls can become their friends and protectors. As such, they require honored spaces, just as an adult would honor power animals or Deities on a more formal altar. In fact, stuffed animals or dolls are very often the focal point for the energy of a specific guide. A parent may wear a Thor's hammer or have a carved eagle on an altar. A child may gain the same energies and benefits from a stuffed lion or a warrior doll.

For a young child, this is an altar. When I was growing up, my altars varied according to my age and what was going on in my life at the time. By the time I reached school age, I had my favorite rocks lined up in a definite way in very specific places around my room. My stuffed animals had their own places on my bed. As I got older, my altars became more sophisticated.

In addition to a personal altar, a family altar is a wonderful way to get everyone involved and co-create something for your home and family. As is true with personal altars, these can be as blatant or as inconspicuous as you choose. The goal is to bring in harmonious and beneficial energies, while honoring the guides and guardians of your home and family.

Each room in our house has its own altar, although some are more obvious than others. But somewhere in each room, you will find a combination of rocks, shells, and/or feathers. In one room, a Green Man sculpture stands watch over an ivy plant and some rocks. In another, a crystal bowl of stones is topped off with the Ponderosa Pine cones we collected on a family outing. In another, Green Tara presides over crystals, feathers, and more.

A family altar should be something that does not need to be off-limits to any member of the family, at least once your children are over the everything-in-the-mouth stage. When they are still young, this may preclude the use of anything breakable or anything that holds an emotional significance to you. Children should certainly be taught that altars are not play areas and the objects on them are not toys. But if they feel they are not allowed to touch, the altar becomes the parents' property and loses its connection to the children.

If you do choose to establish a permanent family altar, it may be a good idea to change it slightly according to the season and upcoming holiday. Children love to use the colors, plants, and symbols of the season in play and decoration. It is also important not to force the altar to remain stagnant. Allow it to change and grow with your family.

Your family altar will become a microcosm of your family's spiritual and religious life. As such, it should reflect where you are at any given time. When a child outgrows Big Bird as a spirit guide, that symbol should be replaced with something more applicable and appropriate. When a child reaches their dedication or adulthood rites, add something to the family altar to recognize this special event.

Magical Tools

Although we do have pagan clergy, most pagans are priests and priestesses in their own right. Solitary pagans may perform all of their rituals alone. Even those that belong to a pagan group perform many rituals on their own. As a result, pagans probably possess more ritual and spiritual items as individuals than any other religious group. Pagan kids never cease to amaze me with the interesting and special items they possess.

These are the tools that our children are exposed to at young ages and will often be trained in the use of as they grow older. The tools you use will very according to your tradition. The various uses of certain tools also depend on one's stage in the training of that path. For example, many pagans use drums for recreation these days. Among those following a shamanic path, many can use the drum to facilitate shamanic trance states. However, only those in advanced shamanic training learn to use the drum for divination, healing, invocation, and other magic.

In light of this, I will only discuss those tools that are commonly used by the general pagan community. These are items that most pagan children will be exposed to at an early age and include the drum or rattle, the wand or knife, the chalice, incense and smudge, candles, and oils.

Creating Magical Tools

As is true with anything, creation tends to become more sophisticated with the age of the child. While some families view magical tools as too serious to be played at by children, most families agree that play is the first step in learning and gaining familiarity. The truth is that pagan kids understand the importance and sanctity of ritual tools, no matter how fun or serious the creation.

A child certainly does not need a sharp knife or a crystal chalice, though many older pagan kids have them. A child's blunt knife or toy wand and a plastic cup can bring the same special significance to ritual for children as the real thing does for adults. It also increases their ability to participate, thereby increasing their interest.

In some families and some magical traditions, ritual tools are part of the training process. The creation of tools may be a pre-requisite for various initiations. In these cases, the creation of magical and ritual tools is serious business and there will be definite guidelines to follow. In this book, I will not attempt to outline all of the traditions, tools, techniques, and tests that might accompany this facet of a specific training system.

Incense, smudge, and candles have an almost universal importance to spirituality and religion. However, each of these items requires parental supervision until the child is old enough to be entrusted with the responsibility of fire use. As I wrote earlier, I was in junior high school before I was allowed to burn candles—in glass holders—alone in my room. There are plenty of children who cannot be trusted alone with burning candles even at that age.

Fire is an element that must be respected and treated with caution. All children should be taught the dangers inherent in the use of fire. Children rarely think about potential consequences of their actions and can easily forget or attempt to hide a burning candle. House or brush fires are often the unfortunate result of a lack of education.

Children around the age of two seem to prefer to blow out all the candles rather than play with them. Around three or four, they become fascinated with them. In their bids for independence and attempt to mimic the adults around them, older toddlers develop a real interest in lighting, blowing out, and relighting candles. By the age of seven, many young children find it an exciting adventure to play with matches and candles. They need to learn to stay away from any fire and that the candles are not part of a game. Candles can be a serious part of a ritual.

Candlemaking

Even toddlers can assist in the making of candles, and they gain a great sense of satisfaction from this. You might consider allowing them a small amount of wax to create their own candle, in whatever colors and design they choose. Most craft stores sell wax granules today that make this an easy project to share with children. With these granules and a small bowl, pot or glass, you can create beautiful candles of any design or color combination you desire.

The innate wonder and magic of children's minds makes candle magic truly powerful for them. It makes sense to children that when we write our wishes on a candle and burn it, the magic is released. After all, we make real wishes with each birthday cake. Obviously, this will require varying degrees of parental supervision, but this can be one of the first simple spells you teach your children.

Choose an appropriate color candles together and write or carve key words or symbols into the side of the candle. You may also want to anoint the candle with a special oil. Then charge it with whatever you want to manifest and let it burn all the way down. Bury any remaining wax and let the Earth assist with the spell. The following are some of the most common candle colors and their major associations. See also the associations with the chakra colors given in chapter 5.

White: Similar to a clear crystal in that it can embody any energies

Black: Protection, grounding, banishing

Red: Physical vitality, sexual energy (particularly male), life energy

Rose or Pink: Romantic love, emotional healing, comfort, self-love

Orange: Sexual energy (especially female), decision making, energy, vitality, fertility

Yellow: Manifestation on the physical plane, self-confidence

Blue: Healing, seeking vision, divination, dreamwork, peace, communication

Green: Balance, harmony, general healing, money, success

Purple: Clairvoyance, astral travel, meditation, protection

Gold: The God, the Sun, general healing
Silver: The Goddess, the Moon, psychic
development

Making Oils

Oils are used by pagans in many different ways. Some people use them simply for fragrance, preferring the essential oil to the synthetic chemical-laden commercial perfumes. Others use them for ritual and magic, calling on the properties of the plant the oil was made from. Children should be taught not to drink even essential oils but these are generally safe for children to use and make. However, it is always a good idea to research the herbs you use. There are herbs that should not be used by pregnant women or people with depressed immune systems.

You also may prefer to keep the making of oils as part of the older child's training. This gives children something to aspire to and allows older children and teens something more advanced to participate in, without having to constantly deal with the little ones. A progression of steps in any teaching system increases healthy competition with oneself and a genuine feeling of pride and achievement.

To make a simple essential oil, use approximately one cup of light vegetable oil. Place it in a clean glass jar. Gather approximately one quarter to one third of a cup of the plants you need and soak them in the oil for three days, in a dark place with the jar capped. Using unbleached cheesecloth to filter out the plant parts, pour the oil into a second clean glass jar. Repeat the process three times or until you achieve the degree of scent you desire. This can be a fun exercise in patience for children, but young children should be supervised when using glass containers.

Drums and Rattles

The drum and rattle are widely used for trance induction and to facilitate shamanic journeying. Followers of many paths use drums in ritual to facilitate meditations and to raise energy. They are used for healing, divination, and the invocation of spirits.

Most children love to play with drums and rattles. A tin can covered with rubber on both open ends and a film canister filled with sand are two very inexpensive, very simple instruments that can introduce a child to the use of rhythm in magic. Many drummers, who are also parents, have found that introducing children to drums and/or rattles at a young age encourages them to develop respect, not only for the drum itself but also for other drummers in a circle. We have found that it helps children to maintain their connections to universal energy as they grow up. Furthermore, when used correctly, drumming can facilitate the healthy release of emotions.

I use the drum regularly for fun, journeying, and healing, as well as for the release of tension, anger, even sadness. When our son was younger and had difficulty verbalizing his feelings, he would play his drum when he was angry or upset. The goal with this type of drumming is not to force any particular rhythm, but rather to allow the energy of the emotion to flow through you. Allow the drum to speak for you. The drum grounds and releases this energy as it purifies both your personal energy field and the space around you. This is beneficial for all children, but may be particularly useful during puberty when emotions are rampant and the child may not always be able to talk easily about his or her feelings.

If you choose to purchase drums for your children, I recommend that you begin with small, simple drums for very young children. As they grow and learn to respect the drum, they gain the ability to care properly for a larger or more expensive drum. If drumming continues to hold their interest as they grow up, then you might purchase a better drum for them—or help them make one on their own.

Through encouraging children to experiment and create their own sacred objects, parents prepare them for life in many ways. You support the healthy development of their self-confidence and ability to problem-solve. You teach them very basic scientific method as you bolster their abilities to combine intuition and creativity with physical manifestation and analytical thinking. This facilitates the development of creativity and real intelligence.

Consecrating Magical Tools

The consecration and use of magical tools is what sets them apart from everyday items. These are tools that were crafted for a specific purpose and have been ritually dedicated to that purpose. This is something that children generally find very easy to understand. This makes these objects special. Children recognize that these tools are not toys and therefore require additional care.

As is true with any ritual involving children, consecration rituals should be designed to be as simple and short as possible while retaining the necessary power. It is also a good idea to involve some sort of physical action in the rituals; something to get kids interested and fully involved. Below I have outlined a simple and generally non-denominational consecration ritual that is intended for use as a guide. It is my hope that this will spark your own creativity and that of your children as you design an appropriate ritual for your own family.

Tool Consecration Ritual

Older children should be encouraged to perform this ritual alone or take the lead in the ceremony. However, all children should be supervised through their first rituals for guidance and support. Guide younger children as appropriate without interfering or attempting to do everything for them.

Have anointing oil or a bowl of sagebrush ready on the altar.

Begin with the smudging ceremony to purify yourself and your child, the altar, the tool to be consecrated, and the surrounding space.

Create sacred space or cast the Circle in your usual manner.

Call upon the Spirits of the directions, the helping spirits of the child, and any Deities the child or family works with. Ask that these beings guide and assist you in this rite. Request their blessings and their acceptance of this special tool.

Holding the anointing oil between both hands, offer it first to the Gods and the spirits. Then anoint the tool with a small amount of the oil, saying as you do so that you are anointing this tool; you bless it and prepare it for consecration by the Gods.

If you are using sagebrush, hold the bowl up to the Gods and spirits first. Then sprinkle a small amount over the tool, saying as you do so that you bless and purify this tool in preparation for consecration by the Gods. Spread the sagebrush around to anoint the entire surface of a drumhead. Then return the sagebrush to the bowl.

Take up the tool and hold it with both hands. Beginning at your root chakra, bring the tool up through all your chakras, attuning it to your personal energy.

Hold the tool up to the Gods and the spirits. Speak from the heart but be sure to make it clear that you have created/chosen this as your working tool. Ask the blessings of the spirits and the Gods for all that you do with this tool. Ask that universal energy may flow freely through you and that you may be divinely inspired when working with this tool. Promise to treat it with respect as a working partner and to use it only for the highest good of all.

For a younger child, it is best to end the ritual at this point. An older child may prefer to stay in Circle and perform a meditation or simply sit in silence, attuning to the newly consecrated tool and receiving any messages that may come through.

Make sure that children keep newly consecrated tools near them, at least at night, for the next few weeks. This will reinforce the bond between child and tool and will further harmonize the tool with the child's personal energy.

Honoring the Spirits

The spirits I refer to in this section include any non-physical beings that you work with in your path. They may take the form of ancestors, Gods and Goddesses, fairy folk, power animals, or any helping spirits. Certainly, the ways in which you work with and honor these beings will vary according to the type of being, your personal preference, and your tradition. In this chapter, I will focus on some common ways that pagans honor their spirits.

Offerings are probably the most powerful and the most common means of honoring the spirits. This crosses all cultural boundaries and is as ancient as humankind's awareness of these spirits. Offerings can be as simple or as elaborate as you choose. An offering should not be seen as a bribe or a plea. It is a continuation of the flow of mutually beneficial energy that honors those who give to us.

Since ancient times, humans have offered sacred herbs, beverages, and foods in thanks for the blessings of the Earth. In ritual, we may also offer a sprinkling of wine, mead, or vodka. We may light candles as an offering and a blessing. It is fairly common for the first and best portions of a meal to be set aside and given to the spirits of the family or place. And many people still leave out a bowl of milk for the fairies.

While many pagans still engage in many of these forms of offerings, modern pagans have become more innovative in their offerings. Some offer water to plants in drought or desert areas. Others collect food and old clothes for donation to the homeless or other needy people. Many volunteer our time at many different organizations or stop to help stray or injured animals. Most work toward peace, tolerance, and harmony with our world and all peoples in some way. And nearly all offer back pure, unconditional energy in our every action. Simply living one's life in a sacred and honest manner is an offering of the highest kind.

These are concrete ways in which children can get involved in offering something back for the blessings they have received. These types of offerings teach children that they can make a difference in the world; that they are not simply victims, though they may not win all the time. These offerings also offer an opportunity for children to experience many people and situations that they may not ordinarily come in contact with. These are rare occasions for growth on many levels of being.

The Give-Away

At least once each year, my family performs a Give-Away. We give away anything from old clothes to food to volunteer time. Volunteer time can take many forms. Anything that gives something back to the planet or the community is ideal: from time spent reading to challenged children or serving meals at food kitchens to planting trees.

The actual physical Give-Away can be seen as a type of medicine. It is something of ours that we freely release and offer to others for their own pleasure and benefit. In this way, the energy is free to move throughout the community and the planet bringing balance, happiness, and abundance to all. This process is a means for us to accept our roles in the great Web of Life and to integrate the understanding that we will be taken care of as long as we remain in that flow.

In modern society we can get so focused on ourselves and our own problems that our communities suffer. In looking out for Number One, we may lose sight of the needs of others, including those of our ecosystems. The Give-Away is a ritual recognition that all our needs are related. The process of Give-Away takes us outside of ourselves and allows a more expanded, less personal view of our situations.

Once we have collected or determined what it is we will give away, we bring that into the Give-Away ceremony. If we are donating time, we bring the image and intent into ceremony. If there are specific Deities related to our donations, they are invoked at the beginning of the ritual. Then, in the middle of the ritual, we consecrate the donations (including image and intent). We bless them all with the highest good for all involved, that everyone who contacts these gifts may be blessed. We ask that these gifts restore balance and be accepted as thanks for all we have received so that the cycle of blessings may continue.

The most important thing about the Give-Away is that it does not simply end with the end of the ritual. We have to handle the practical aspects of how to carry out the giving of our offerings. We must actually follow through and complete what we have intended. This is an excellent lesson for children in keeping promises and following through on actions. [i]

Personal Creativity

Artwork, music, dance, and writing can be extremely beneficial for children. Opening up to one's own inner Self and to one's helping spirits through creativity of any form is a tremendous honoring. Children should be encouraged to draw, paint, write, create music, or be creative in their own ways.

You may be quite surprised by their creations when children are working directly with the spirits. I have never been a great artist in terms of painting and drawing. But beginning around the age of ten, I have created some truly inspired drawings of Deities and power animals simply through allowing them to work through me. Most of the time, I slipped into trance and was not aware that I was opening to anyone. But the drawings that resulted could never have been created by my overly analytical Self.

This is also how I write, and I strongly encourage children to write poetry or stories or rituals if they have any desire to do so. Often I will edit a story or chapter and wonder who really wrote it. It is obvious when I am trying to pull a book or article out of my own mind and when it flows through me. Writing can be very similar to the scrying method given earlier and it may develop into automatic writing, in which spirit guides come through with messages for the child.

Children love to play with clay. If drawing and writing don't seem to be doing it for your child, get out the clay and allow him to sculpt along with you. Put on some music and light some incense. Then just let your imaginations run wild without any critique of your creations.

As children grow up, they will be more able to understand the value in creating statues honoring the spirits that work with them. Unfortunately, as children get older and assimilate into society, they tend to become more analytical, often blocking the free flow of that creativity. Parents of older children may have special considerations when encouraging the development of personal creativity in their kids. You may need to develop a good deal of patience and creativity in order to assist your children in re-establishing that link to their innate creativity.

If this is your situation, I recommend starting out very simply. You might begin by creating symbols in clay or on paper. Making amulets can be a fun and easy way to get the creative juices flowing. However, there is another form of sculpture that I recommend for anyone. This is sculpture made from found objects. I highly recommend it for these types of situations because it encourages children to begin to see potential in the world around them, including old junk.

This type of sculpture is highly symbolic. It can take any form the child desires, provided it speaks to the child in some way. The idea that the sculpture starts out as junk eliminates a lot of the pressure to create beautiful pieces of art and refocuses attention on the creative process. In one sense this is great therapy. In another sense, it can allow children's intuitive doors to open just enough for the spirits to begin to work with them.

Junk Walk

Begin by gathering things like glue, string, wire, clay, or anything else that may possibly be needed to hold your found objects together or serve as a base for them. Then go out on a Junk Walk. If you are taking young children with you, they should be supervised to prevent injury. All ages are likely to enjoy this type of walk, but it is recommended more for older children and teenagers.

Take a bag with you and pick up whatever catches your attention. Trust that you will pick up whatever you need and then some. If there is a specific spirit or issue that you would like to focus on, sit in silent meditation before going out on the walk. Hold it in your mind as you walk.

When you return from your walk, dump everything out onto the floor or a large working table. Take a short break, if you wish, but then move directly into your creation. Feel free to experiment. Dismantle anything that doesn't feel right and start over. Keep in mind that someone else may have been guided to pick up something for you. It is permissible to ask to use objects that another person brought home. It should also be ok to say no to such a request.

It may help to work with some light music on, speaking as little as possible. However, if the talking flows easily and does not detract from the creative process, it may be just the thing to keep the analytical mind occupied while the spirit and body-mind create.

Depending on the child, this may flow immediately or it may take some time. Make this a safe and fun exercise and the child may feel comfortable enough to stick with it. Even if they do not want to try this exercise again, they will benefit greatly from your lack of judgment and unconditional love.

Many people today feel turned off by the very idea of a "religion." This is often a reaction to negative experiences with some of the organized religions that attempt to control followers. These people reject the importance placed on politics rather than honest spiritual beliefs, and this can color their view of religion itself.

It is important that pagan kids understand that religion does not have to be like that. Religion in its highest form is simply the honoring and working with our helping spirits. While we may prefer to call this spirituality, in reality that line is not so finely drawn.

Children may not have a specific label for their religion or spirituality, but that is not important. Many pagans tend to resist labels because they tend to be limiting. If children learn to walk in honor and respect for all life and to strive toward self-knowledge, they may label themselves Pumpkinheads if they choose. What matters is how this affects them and their lives. If our children grow up happy and healthy, then our "religion" has served its purpose.

i.   Much of the section on the Give-Away is reprinted exactly as it first appeared in the *InnerConnexion*, Litha 1998 issue.

Chapter 11
Honesty vs. Secrecy

Honesty is one of the most vital characteristics of a healthy family. Without honesty, there is no trust. Without honesty, there is no confidence in Self or others. But within pagan families, honesty outside the immediate family, particularly regarding spirituality, can be an extremely sensitive issue. It is a sad fact that there are many pagans who cannot even be fully honest about their spiritual beliefs within their immediate families.

As wonderful as it was to have been raised outside mainstream religion, there was a down side for me, and for every other child raised like me. I learned the importance of secrecy at a very young age and began to live a double life. Even now that the New Age movement has become big business and paganism is on the rise, we are still not readily accepted by dominant society.

Kids growing up in metaphysical homes today still deal with the same conflicts, although often to a lesser degree. There is tremendous pressure on children to conform in order to make friends and avoid taunting. Children also have less available options for escape than adults do. They cannot move to a new area, change jobs, or socialize superficially with one group while having real friends in another area, particularly those that attend school.

This raises the question of whether to be totally honest or to pretend to be like everyone else. It is a question faced daily by anyone on the fringes of the majority. Children often have an instinctual desire to be honest with people, particularly friends. Oddly enough, children who were not raised pagan are often more likely to be open about the pagan exploration of their family than are children who were raised pagan from birth. It is an exciting new development that they naturally want to share with others.

However, in order to function in society, complete honesty and openness are not always possible. We all play a variety of roles throughout our lives. Each role is tailored to the situation at hand. Furthermore, many of our public roles may be in direct conflict with our more private roles.

The Roles We Play

The difficulty arises when roles that are meant to be shared openly become necessarily restricted. For example, the role of friend should be relatively open. Children growing up with metaphysical beliefs will often not share this side of themselves with mainstream friends for fear of rejection and ridicule. This puts the relationship at a disadvantage from the beginning. As a result, pagan children have even more roles to play and more reason to keep these roles separate.

A large part of one's public role is deciding what should be encompassed within that role. For most followers of mainstream religions, this is not even a question that comes to mind. Unless the individual is extremely devout, religion is not often a part of their public persona. They neither hide it nor broadcast it. It is like skin color, hair color, or anything else that is an integral part of who we are without needing to think about it.

This may be a good perspective for many pagan families to develop. Then the major focus of discussions can be on things like whether or not to correct assumptions regarding your religion, how to handle direct questions, and when the public persona should give way to the private friend and family persona.

Support Systems

Having some form of pagan community to associate with makes living with these issues much easier. It can provide an invaluable support system for families that have none. Within a pagan (or pagan-friendly metaphysical) community, your children may be able to interact with other children who are following the same or similar spiritual paths as their own. There is also the opportunity for interaction with older pagan children who may serve as role models.

These communities often become a sub-culture within the larger community where we live and work. Among these people, our children do not need to be careful about what they say and to whom. A community may develop out of a Grove or coven, even a study or meditation group. These communities generally follow the same path, but will certainly stress acceptance of diversity.

Another type of pagan community is the festival community, described in chapter 7. These may or may not be extensions of a local community. Festivals, especially the outdoor gatherings, are a unique experience. They frequently become a sort of world within the world, where everyone is pagan and accepting of pagan values and traditions. People share their thoughts, feelings, and practices.

Within the children's and teen groups that are so popular at festivals, the children often decide on their own speakers, fire circles, and discussions. Often, these discussions focus on issues that particularly affect children of that age, including the questions of sexuality and openness regarding their spirituality.

I strongly support these types of discussion groups, whether at festivals or elsewhere, and have been greatly honored to facilitate them at festivals around the country. They give children an opportunity to see first-hand that they are not alone in their feelings and experiences. Kids are free to share with peers who understand and they can often trade ideas on how to handle what may come up. In learning to act with integrity, children need to think for themselves and gather information so that they may make informed decisions. However, decisions regarding this type of honesty must also be discussed with the family, if these decisions have the potential to affect others in the family.

The friendships that develop at festivals can be extremely important and long-term. Even if the friends only see each other at that one festival each year, the relationship can become a lifeline for a child who does not know any local pagan kids. In truth, these friendships are important even to children who have local pagan playgroups. These children share a bond of spirituality, freedom, and bonding over a weekend or week.

Although we participate in a local pagan playgroup, our son stays in touch with some of the boys he meets each year at a Mabon festival. They speak on the phone and email each other frequently. If my teaching travels take us near these friends, we make it a point to get together to reinforce the friendships. They may not have seen each other for over a year but when they get together, they click as if they just saw each other last week. They discuss religion and relationships in a surprisingly philosophical way and those kinds of friendships are rare.

Solitary Families

Unfortunately, not every pagan family has access to a pagan community, or for some reason they are unable to interact with the local community. The feeling of isolation can be very difficult on both parents and children in the absence of some form of support system. This takes a great deal more family creativity and closeness. It requires open communication and support within the family.

When my parents were children, this was not an issue. These things were not discussed outside the home. When I was a child, the silence had been broken by the 1960s. Many people flaunted alternate beliefs and activities. However, anyone that explored alternative lifestyles was still thought of as foolish, or worse, by the vast majority of mainstream people. This perception made life very difficult for children like me.

Although we have much to thank the New Age movement for, pagan paths are still misunderstood and feared by many. Things have changed, but they have not changed so much that children no longer need to think first before telling someone about their Samhain celebration. I know from my own experience how difficult it is to be without a pagan community.

This situation fosters a bond between family members that is very special. As parents of pagan children without a supportive community, you have it a bit more difficult. Not only must you handle your own feelings of loneliness but you also must create a supportive family atmosphere. It is up to you to guide your children through, whether you choose to be open about your spirituality or not.

Being Out

Being open about a pagan path can be very liberating for an adult who is not afraid for their job, home, or standing in the community. After years of living a double life, it has been a sometimes tense but mainly freeing feeling to be open about who I am. However, when we decided to have a child, this issue required a great deal of thought that will continue until our son is out on his own.

Parents do need to consider what is best for their children. Our actions have a definite impact on our children. Once we accept the responsibility to be parents, we are parents, no matter what role we are living at the moment. Even if we are not interacting with our children, or are miles away, how we live our lives affects how our children view the world. It also has more power to affect their behavior than many of us want to believe.

However, it is a fact that having to think about this issue will often bring up related issues for parents that they may have repressed. It is important that the parents handle their own issues before making any decisions for their children. Unresolved issues have a way of controlling us without our knowledge.

This is part of the personal shadow side. While the shadow side holds all of our hidden strengths, it is also that place where we hide away all of those things we do not want the world to see. It contains memories, beliefs, and fears that we don't want to have to face or do not want to admit are a part of our inner selves.

Shadow aspects only gain more power over us when they are submerged in the unconscious. While we are no longer consciously aware of them, they continue to influence our lives, leaving us feeling like victims or out of control. They create a filter through which we make decisions and experience the world. Consequently, any decisions we make as parents with unresolved issues in those areas may not be the most enlightened or the most beneficial decisions we could make.

For example, I have known pagan parents who were terrified that someone outside the pagan community would discover they were pagan. They avoided meeting other pagans in public and some even kept their religion a secret from their children. These children were terribly hurt and confused when they reached an age where their parents felt they could keep the secret and told them the truth. Many children who were aware of the family religion but were isolated from community because of parental fears grew up with feelings of embarrassment and shame.

I have also known pagan parents who decided that they needed to be totally open about their religion and demanded the same of their children. These were occasionally people who had decided for various reasons to be blatantly pagan in all situations. Some of these children were even berated or punished for not wearing religious jewelry to school or for not being fully open with a neighbor.

These are certainly extreme situations and are relatively uncommon. For most parents, the best decisions lie somewhere in the middle. But I offer these examples to illustrate how we can unconsciously project our own issues onto our children. Rather than accepting their individuality and their right to choose for themselves within reason, we may have expectations of them that are based solely on our own shadow stuff. We need to examine continually our own motives for our actions.

I cannot say what choices are the best for anyone else's family. Each family must find their own way and make the best decisions they can at the time. It is important to keep in mind that these decisions may change with time and that is perfectly normal. The decision to be open about an 'alternative' spirituality may depend on a number of factors, including region, neighborhood, jobs, and many more.

Whatever we decide, it is important not to bash other religions or belittle others for making different choices. If our children are to avoid the destructive paths taken by many of those who would discriminate against pagans, they must be wiser and more centered in their own higher selves. The cycles of violence and oppression do not end by the minority, who may be gaining ground, indulging in the same behaviors as their oppressors.

Children need to know that many of oppressive or hostile people do not know any better—not that this is a reason to tolerate their behavior. But most of these people are afraid and ignorant. They are reacting through thousands of years of indoctrinated dogma and their lack of ability to think for themselves. If we are to create a happier, healthier reality, we need to set the example.

In making these types of decisions for your family, it is important to think it through fully and get clear on all the factors involved. Parents need to protect their children. As a result, parents can desire to protect their kids from issues that they know have the potential to cause them pain. But in doing so, parents may become overly protective, insulating children too much from real life issues that they will have to face sooner or later.

In an earlier chapter, I described my young friend who lost her lover at college as the result of his parents' reaction to her spirituality. Sad as this is, it is a possibility for anyone outside mainstream religion. To be honest, it is a potential issue for anyone dating outside a specific religion, mainstream or not.

This young woman's parents expressed what most parents feel when something like this happens to our children. "It would have been easier if she broke her arm instead of her heart. As a parent, we hurt as bad as they do and it is tough to say 'these things happen and it won't hurt as bad in time.' That sucks as an explanation." Indeed, it does. It is even more difficult when a child is hurt because someone fears their religion or skin color or anything else that does not necessarily define who one is.

As difficult as it may be, parents need to be strong and control their often overwhelming need to protect. Unless they are prepared to change their religion or spiritual beliefs to conform to mainstream society, they must prepare their children to handle this before they are out on their own. Parents do them a disservice by hiding this reality. Nor do parents support their children by believing that they will always encounter difficult situations. There are many people who are very openly pagan and have little or no problems with neighbors or strangers.

It is interesting to note that most young people are far more accepting of pagan paths than their parents, as illustrated by the situation with my young friend in college. While their impressions are often colored by media representations of pagan paths, the media has been much more glamorizing, if not realistic, in recent years. As a result, many young people think it is cool or exciting that a friend or a friend's family member is pagan. This still requires educating these young people, but our children are getting a head start by the increasingly beneficial perceptions of certain pagan paths.

Family Discussions

You can prepare your children by maintaining safe and open communication in the family. It is usually best to avoid bringing up the extreme examples unless they are a reality in your lives. You might also try asking leading questions but allowing children to suggest ways to handle potential or real situations. Not only does this empower them to problem-solve at young ages, it also evokes some surprisingly inspired ideas.

Beginning in the toddler years, it can be useful to engage the help of older siblings, friends, or other young relatives. The young child who tags along after an older child will naturally imitate the words and actions of the older child. Older siblings, in particular, become like gods to the young child. I know one boy who followed his older sister everywhere. If she said, "Let's play a game and pretend," he was right there acting the part. When she said, "Keep this a secret," his lips were sealed.

Whether you prefer secrecy, openness, or somewhere in between, this is a definite option for many parents. Children of any age also tend to view parents and most adults as authority figures. Even in a good parent-child relationship, some children may feel more comfortable hearing the facts of life from a sibling or friend. Suggestions or directives about how the family is going to handle certain situations may be more easily accepted and followed if another, preferably older and respected, child is included in the discussion.

An older relative or friend can speak to the child on his or her level. This older child may be able to relate applicable personal experience. If handled well, this has the potential to make the discussion more than a parent-child talk. While family is very important to a child, peers also may have the power to affect their decisions and behavior.

Rather than limit this to a one-time talk, it is much more effective if time is set aside for general family discussions on a regular basis. It is your responsibility as the parent to keep your finger on the pulse of your family in a sense. It is very important that you develop a feel for how often these talks need to happen and how deep they should be. They should be regular enough that emotions do not build to a difficult point but not so often that your family feels suffocated.

If you have the time to get together for nightly or weekly dinners, these conversations can be as casual or as serious as they need to be, without allowing dinners to become arguments. In this way, the small things that tend to build can be discussed and handled quickly. If something comes up at a dinner or other casual conversation more than once, or if there is a serious emotional charge, this should be brought up at a separate discussion.

Keeping the serious discussions separate is a very important point. No one likes to be put on the spot, especially during a family meal. One child may be fine with airing his or her feelings with the entire family. Other children may prefer to keep these talks between them and their parents or with one particular parent.

Our son tends to discuss serious issues with me, mainly because we spend nearly all of our time together. Each parent has a unique relationship with his or her children, and this should not be seen as a preference for one parent over the other. These relationships also have a way of changing over time. I handle each issue as soon as possible after it occurs. We began having conversations about differing religions when he was just three. As he gets older, his thoughts and feelings regarding how to handle questions or ignorance become more sophisticated. Now he decides, with my full support, how to handle questions from non-pagan neighborhood kids.

When our son was seven, he asked me if he had to be completely honest when neighborhood kids ask him if he goes to church. I asked what he meant and what he wanted to say (or had said). He wanted to know if he had to tell them that we are pagan. Well, of course not! He decided that, in most cases, he would answer the question truthfully without offering any additional information. There are some kids he feels comfortable telling and others he does not. Of course, he makes no effort to hide his altars no matter who comes over to play. We support his choices completely.

Obviously, your family discussions will not be limited to the issues of this chapter. However, when faced with these types of issues, it is even more important that our children feel the support and strength of the family. They need to know that they are not alone and that they can share their feelings, fears, and successes with someone who honestly cares. This can make all the difference in the world to a child who cannot share his spirituality with anyone outside the family.

With that in mind, you can eliminate the need for a set time and formal discussion by maintaining your own open communication and mutual trust with each of your children. Children who know that they are a parent's top priority and that they will be able to talk openly whenever it is necessary feel much more confident and secure.

Bedtime is frequently a perfect time to share and talk. When it is quiet and we are trying to get to sleep, our minds tend to go over the events of the day. Difficult events can end up in a kind of loop, preventing sleep. Journal keeping is a great way to work through these issues, but it is not for every child. It is obviously not an option for the very young.

In the dark at bedtime, small things may become big monsters, working up our emotions and preventing restful sleep. Big issues become even more imposing and can appear impossible to overcome. The many unique issues facing pagan children can often be effectively defused, or at least diminished, through this very simple bedtime sharing. All you need to do is to be there without pushing. Allow conversation to flow forth spontaneously and accept that quite often your child may need the closeness of your loving energy without discussion.

The Legality of Religion and Spirituality

If you read any pagan magazines or newsletters, you are aware that plenty of pagans have encountered problems with ignorant communities and legal actions, ranging from police at the door to custody battles. We do need to be aware of—and prepared for—these possibilities. But keep in mind that most pagans have not encountered these types of situations.

This is a generalization and the potential for police or other legal involvement will largely depend on your area and your practices. However, those pagans who are bringing pagan businesses into certain neighborhoods or are involved in divorce and custody battles, need to know their rights. These are most often the pagans who end up in court over their beliefs.

Rather than the choice being forced on us, it is far more likely that we will be the ones to decide whether or not publicly to fight for the protection of our rights. You may want to get your religious holidays off at work and your child's school. Or you may choose to fight to keep the Ten Commandments from being posted in public places. The sad truth is that many people in the majority culture do not recognize our practices as valid "religions." And those who do may feel that our religions should be outlawed.

Article 18 of the United Nations Universal Declaration on Human Rights states that, "Everyone has the right to freedom of thought, conscience, and religion. This right includes freedom to change his religion or belief, and freedom, either alone or in community with others and in public or private, to manifest his religion or belief in teaching, practice, worship, and observance." [i]

In America, we can look to the First and Fourteenth Amendments of the United States Constitution. Most of us realize that Wicca is a formally recognized religion and therefore protected as such under Constitutional law. The first real lawsuit to set this important precedent was Dettmer v Landon in 1985. In this case, the District Court of Virginia ruled that Witchcraft is a legitimate religion and falls within a recognizable religious category. In 1986, J. Butzner upheld this decision in Federal Appeals court.

But what about those of us who are not Wiccan? While many people think of pagan as Wiccan, this is not necessarily the case. The terms *Pagan* and *Heathen* includes a great many paths from Druidry and shamanism to Santeria and Asatru, and many more, including a huge number of "unlabeled" pagans.

Do we all have the same rights?

Yes!

In addition to those rights guaranteed by the United Nations, Americans have the freedom of religious belief, as well as the right to freedom of speech and peaceful assembly. To be protected, as a religious belief under United States federal law, it must be sincerely held and perceived by the individual as religious.

Canadians have the right to freedom of thought, belief, opinion, and expression, as well as the right to peaceful assembly and association, according to Article II of the Canadian Charter of Rights and Freedoms. Many other countries have similar rights. It would be beneficial for you to look into the rights guaranteed to you by the United Nations and the particular country in which you reside.

What we do in our own homes (within reason) is further protected by the United States Constitution. The First Amendment guarantees all citizens the right to be secure against unreasonable searches and seizures. This means that no one can come search your home, person, or vehicle without probable cause, supported by "oath or affirmation," and a warrant.

It is true that many states and cities have enacted more stringent laws regarding what you can do where. For example, to assemble for any purpose in a public place may require a permit. These laws vary from state to state and it is your responsibility to know when the rules change. It is also true, at least according to U.S. Constitutional Amendment Fourteen, that no state can enact a law abridging or violating these guaranteed privileges and immunities. However, it is in everyone's best interests to get informed and know exactly what your rights are in any given place.

There are some issues that we pagans may disagree with but still are held accountable for if we are caught. The possession of animal parts is one of these. While many pagans would never kill for an animal's fur or plumage, most of us have no idea where the feathers in a smudge fan or the fur on a staff really came from.

As followers of Earth-honoring spiritualities, we need to recognize that there are many people who hunt or illegally capture wild animals to sell fur, feathers, and other body parts. In light of this, we only honor ourselves, our Deities, and our animal allies, by finding out what animal the feathers or fur came from and how they were obtained. Sad as it may be, the laws regarding possession of feathers and body parts of certain animals are in place to protect the species of concern. The law enforcement officials do not know whether you picked that feather up off the ground or killed the bird to obtain it.

Unless you have specific permits, you are not permitted to have any part of an endangered or threatened animal. You are also not legally allowed to possess the feathers of most wild birds. Most native wildlife is protected and there are many species for whom hunting permits are never issued. Check with both federal and state governments if you want to know what creatures are not protected.

Certainly, most people have collections of feathers they have found on the ground. But if you are buying feathers, please find out where they came from. I won't pretend that all pagans will simply obey the laws and not keep or purchase any questionable feathers. So, if you are going to obtain them, please try to receive molted feathers.

The possession of what mainstream society may term "weapons" is another contentious issue with many pagans. It is illegal in many places to carry a weapon, particularly a concealed weapon. Athames, swords, other knives, etc are all considered weapons and therefore potentially dangerous. The possession of these ritual items may result in a ticket or other legal action, particularly if you choose to carry them into a public place.

This is a difficult topic. Many pagan gatherings, especially the hotel conferences, have their own rules in place to avoid liabilities and be permitted to return to the hotel for another event. This is simply a fact of life in the modern world. Wishing it away won't do you much good. Furthermore, there are plenty of dangerous or unstable people who really should not be carrying any form of weapon into a public place. And many of these would pretend to be pagan if it would allow them to possess such items legally.

Knives and swords are an integral part of many pagan paths. They are sacred ritual items. Our children are taught to respect and work with these items properly. I would recommend you also teach your children about the laws pertaining to their use and possession so they might make informed choices.

Some pagans have gotten into a fair amount of legal trouble by carrying knives out in the open or by being utterly blatant about hiding them. Most of those I have been aware of received a summons for more than simple possession of a weapon. We need to be aware of our own behavior and the possible projection of our own fears of oppression.

I do not mean to place all the blame on pagans. To be honest, I have had my share of difficulties with the police and other "authority" figures. But for the most part, it is true that we receive the kind of energy that we send out. If we think of the police as beings, just like us, who are seeking happiness, joy, and meaning in life, we can treat them with the respect they deserve as humans.

This type of attitude has gotten me out of some close calls. If nothing else, it can prevent a bad situation from getting worse and shows that pagans are not a bunch of rude, out of control fools.

Drugs and alcohol can be a very touchy subject for some pagans. It is another issue that we need to be very careful about while examining our own motives for certain actions. Pagans tend to be very adamant about their freedom, and can be rather anarchist in their philosophies. They don't generally like authority or hierarchy and prefer to live in a circle of equals with everyone being self-responsible. As a result, they may object to the legal restrictions on drugs and serving alcohol to minors.

Some pagans may also object to any laws restricting sexuality and children. Sexuality is a great gift, and many pagans feel they honor the union of God and Goddess by engaging in varied sexual encounters. There are pagans who encourage or allow sexual contact between minor children. There are even those who allow this between minor children and adults. This is another controversial topic in pagan communities.

While many pagans are far less afraid and confused about sexuality than the majority culture, we do not want our children to get hurt or contract a sexually transmitted disease. We do not want them to have to experience an unwanted pregnancy and all that entails. It is a parent's responsibility to decide what the boundaries are for their minor children. It is also our responsibility to educate our children about sexuality and what is associated with it.

While some of us may claim that these things are part of our religion, few neo-pagan religions require the use of sex, alcohol, or drugs. As far as I know, none require that minor children either ingest these substances or participate in sexual encounters. We need to be aware, when we loudly proclaim that the laws are interfering with our religious freedoms, that there is a difference between what we want and what is actually part of our religions.

We are all striving for respect and acceptance. We do that by choosing our fights wisely, particularly when we have children. Choosing to flaunt legal restrictions and risk ending up in jail might be more wisely reserved for truly important fights, if there is no one to care for our children in our absence. Even if our children can stay with family, we need to consider our actions. We do want our children to learn to stand up for their beliefs and their rights. We want them to see us as strong individuals who live with honor and conviction. But we do not want to be perceived as parents who fought over absolutely everything and put their family's well-being at risk for relatively unimportant fights.

The focus of this chapter is an unfortunate fact of life for pagan families. While no one can give you an easy way around it or tell you absolutely how to handle its effects in your family, you need to know that you are not alone either. Obviously your children have you. However, pagan parents also need to know that there are many of us out there, experiencing many of the same issues.

If you do not have a support system or are a single parent, I strongly recommend that you try to connect with other pagan parents. There are several places for pagan parents to go on the Internet. For those of you without Internet access, there are metaphysical bookstores in most areas and a multitude of publications where you might find classes or groups or even place your own ad.

Circle Magazine is a great place to find pen pals, if secrecy is a high priority for you.

Most importantly, keep in mind that the Gods and the spirits are always there for you when you need Them. You are never truly alone. They will be your support system until you can find one in this reality. And They can help you connect with the right people for you. All you need do is ask. Most of all, know that in raising healthy, loving children, you are contributing to their personal spiritual growth as well as that of our entire society.

i.   Foundation for Religious Freedom Website

Chapter 12
Rites of Passage

A vast number of pagans do not follow a specific magical tradition that dictates how and when rituals must be done. As a result, modern pagans are open to spirit guidance and their own intuition as they design their own rituals. For pagan parents, it becomes even more important to be able to create powerful rituals simply because these new traditions frequently do not spell out for us how it should be done with children.

There are a number of books on the market today that detail elaborate rituals for just about every occasion. If these rituals work well for you and your children as written in a book, that is wonderful. But often people find that something is missing or it just doesn't seem to fit. It is also quite common for your needs to change as you grow into your pagan path. Rituals that may have worked well for you in the beginning may not as you progress along your path.

In these cases, you may prefer to design your own rituals, rather than searching through dozens of books to find one that does fit you. In chapter 6, I offered you a section on designing rituals for kids to help you get started. This is also why the ritual outlines in this book are non-denominational and as open as possible. It is my hope that my ideas will offer you a basic format that will spark your own creativity.

Rites of passage are, by definition, a marking of life changes. They are a ritual acknowledgement of the death of one chapter of life and the birth of another. Today, rites of passage are often superficial excuses to buy cards and presents. In fact, many rites of passage are completely overlooked by the majority of society.

The main point to keep in mind when creating any ritual is to follow your feelings. While many books detail certain elements that should be included, this is not true for all people. If we truly are to empower ourselves to create from our hearts, we need to release those deeply ingrained feelings of "should." Open to yourself, the God and Goddess, and your spirit guides. Go with whatever feels right to you. If that works, that is excellent. If it doesn't, work with it a bit more. You will get it right for you and your children.

If your children are old enough to assist with the creation of their own rituals, you might encourage this. This is especially recommended for the passage into adulthood. Not only is it wonderful training for a pagan child, but children are also less blocked by old and restricting beliefs. As a result they may be able to contribute powerful elements that truly speak to their souls. This is an important factor of any ritual.

The major ritual elements were described in chapter 6. In this chapter, I will focus more on the core of the ritual. The core section in a rite of passage involves an experience and release that is a ritual enactment of the acceptance and integration of this life passage.

The experience and release element is essential to bring the focus of the ritual into reality. Without this portion, the rite is in danger of becoming a mental activity rather than a deep rite of passage. It is necessary for this to be done in a safe space because the emotional charge created may release deep and repressed emotions.

Many rites are designed with some type of ritual action to manifest this element physically. If possible, all of the senses should be activated by this ritual action. Again, we use sensory input to bypass the analytical mind. I have seen many wonderful ritual actions from a cutting of symbolic cords to a purification by fire of photos or pieces of paper with things to release written on them.

The action of the rite makes it absolutely clear that we have the choice of remaining where we are or passing through this symbolic action. We can remain stuck in old patterns or fully experience the rite to break us out of old stuff. This can be a powerful tool for internal change that will manifest as external change once the rite is concluded.

After this great release, most people require closure and grounding of all this energy. This is often part of the Closing and may be accomplished in many ways, from meditation to discussion to asking for support and guidance from spirit guides and Deities. This is the perfect time to use any of the grounding exercises in chapter 4. Through this ritual element, we accept the new phase and our new identities.

Pregnancy

Hopefully, you went through the necessary personal preparation before becoming pregnant. Ideally, you should be certain that you are ready to become a parent and are aware of the changes you can expect through pregnancy and beyond. Even if the pregnancy is a complete surprise, your choice of whether or not to terminate the pregnancy is the result of some serious personal work. Chances are if you are reading this book, you have decided to keep the baby so that is my main focus in this section.

Pregnancy rituals are predominantly designed for the pregnant woman. While fathers-to-be are certainly affected, it is the woman who will experience major life changes during a pregnancy. She is the one whose body and lifestyle have been dramatically altered, and she is the main one who will feel the energetic effects of the incoming spirit.

Some pagan groups may have three separate rituals: one for each trimester. While this is a valid ritual process marking the physical and energetic differences of each of the trimesters, the ritual I have outlined below is simply to honor the fact that a conception has taken place and to ask for blessings throughout the pregnancy and delivery.

Pregnancy Blessing

Set up altar with pastel or Earth colors, flowers, candles. Spring flowers are best, if possible. Include some symbol of the Mother Goddess or the Earth Herself and a Father or Fertility God. Smudge or burn incense. Have ready on the altar blessing oil and any Medicine pouches or other sacred objects for the parents or child.

Create sacred space in your preferred manner.

The ceremonial leader invokes the chosen Gods and Goddesses, the spirit guides of the parents-to-be, the spirit of the incoming child, and any other beings you wish to have present. The leader states the purposes of this rite: that you have gathered to honor _____ (mother/father's names) and celebrate her/their process of becoming a Mother/Father. You have also gathered to celebrate the return of this being to this reality and his or her entrance into your family. Ask the guidance and protection of those invoked during this ritual and beyond, that your every action may honor them.

The ceremonial leader anoints the mother/father with the blessing oil, saying that you bless these individuals with wisdom, patience, compassion, strength, and anything else you feel an ideal parent would embody.

The ceremonial leader thanks the incoming spirit on behalf of everyone present for choosing this family, for his or her presence in your lives, and for sharing his or her Earth journey with you.

Go around the circle (or go back and forth between mother and father if no one else is present) three times offering prayers for an easy and healthy pregnancy and an easy, safe delivery.

The gifts are blessed and any sacred items are charged with the intent of this celebration.

First the mother (then the father, if present) goes before each quarter, presenting herself as a mother-to-be and asks the blessings and protection of the Spirits of the directions. She (with the father, if present) then presents herself to Father Sky, Mother Earth, and the Great Spirit at the center of the Circle. She (they) asks for Their blessings and Their guidance and protection along this new path. She (they) promises to raise this child in honor and to teach him/her respect for All Life.

The mother/parents return to the circle. The ceremonial leader instructs everyone to hold a single thought in their minds, perhaps a happy, healthy baby and family or the total focus of the ritual. Participants are directed to hold this thought as everyone intones the *Om*. Maintain the intonation until you feel the energy has built enough. The leader will give a sign and everyone should yell, releasing the thought into the universe.

Ground and center in your preferred manner.

The leader thanks and releases all beings invoked and closes the ritual.

Abortion

I include this section because many parents must deal with pregnant teenagers and abortion is frequently the decision in these situations. Any woman who has carried a child or had an abortion will tell you, it is not simply a physical choice. This is not a decayed tooth that must be removed and discarded. Hormones and emotions are present that cannot be ignored or suppressed.

In order for the woman truly to move forward from this event, these emotions must be dealt with in a loving and supportive manner. And while we may say that we perceive it as simply an embryo or fetus that has been eliminated, few women who have been through it honestly feel that way. It was a potential child and should be treated as such in an appropriate ritual, whether or not a spirit was ready to enter the body.

Energetic healing can be vital or the resultant damage to associated chakras can cause additional problems, including additional unwanted pregnancies. However, unless you are proficient in energetic healing techniques, I would recommend using the Drum Purification Ceremony, spending as much time as is need at each chakra, with particular concentration on first, second, and heart chakras. Follow this up with some extra nurturing of the woman-child who had the abortion, as well as some in-depth discussions to determine why she created this. I also recommend that she engage in some private journaling.

I should also point out that this ritual is easily adapted for the young man whose girlfriend or partner has had an abortion. These young men frequently experience similar emotional and energetic trauma that cannot be ignored. Unfortunately, their pain is often overlooked for many reasons. They may need ritual clearing and family support as much as the young woman does.

This ritual should be done in private with only the girl and her mother, or both parents if she feels comfortable with the presence of her father. If possible, the girl should be the one to lead the ritual. Parents are present for energetic and emotional support.

No special preparation is required for this ritual. However, any child who has need of an abortion that was not the result of a rape should at the very least receive counseling in the use of contraceptives and the facts about sexually transmitted diseases. I would also recommend some form of therapy (not necessarily professional or mainstream) to get to the root of why she created this in the first place and how to clear those causes before they bring her even more suffering.

If this pregnancy was the result of a rape, focus on the release of pain and suffering as well as any guilt she may feel. Make nurturing and restoring a feeling of security top priorities. Then follow up by getting her some form of counseling.

Abortion Healing

Set up altar with dark colors, especially dark red and black. Try to have some representation of the Maiden and Mother aspects of the Goddess as well as a single hard-boiled egg. If this ritual cannot take place outside, also have a small pot of earth, larger than the egg. Smudge or burn incense (myrrh is recommended).

Create sacred space in your preferred manner.

If the girl is able, she invokes the chosen Gods and Goddesses, her spirit guides, and any other beings you wish to have present. This is a good time to call upon the Dark Goddesses as well as the lighter ones. It is They who will need to show your daughter how to be with the darkness of her shadow and to pass through the emotion of this time so that the light aspects can lead her back to herself.

227

State the purpose of this rite—that you have come before the Gods, Goddesses, and your helping spirits to release the pain and suffering of the abortion along with those things that brought you to this point. You should also state quite honestly what those things may be and take responsibility for your actions. Ask their guidance and protection during this ritual and beyond that your every action may honor them.

Pick up the Mother Goddess symbol. Tell Her everything you are feeling and ask for Her blessings. Tell Her that you recognize that you are not ready to be a mother and promise to be very careful about contraception or abstinence in the future. Do not make promises you do not intend to keep.

Pick up the Maiden symbol and speak to Her. Tell Her that now you are somewhere between Maiden and Mother. While you will never be the same child again, ask Her help in finding your way back to your joy in your youth.

Sit comfortably on the floor or a chair and allow your mother or parents to take over the ritual. At this point, the mother or parents should perform some form of healing on their daughter together. This may be the Drum Purification Ceremony, an energy sending, or simply a big family hug, as you send all your unconditional love into your daughter. Be certain that any judgments or resentment are left outside the Circle. Follow this up by telling her how much you love her and how proud you are of her. Tell her of the strength, courage, etc. that you see in her.

Allow as much time as is necessary for the free flowing of emotion.

Ground and center in your preferred manner.

The daughter will take over the ritual by taking up the hard-boiled egg. Speak to any spirit that may have been waiting to enter your womb and apologize for the confusion. Send it your love and say that when you are ready you would welcome that spirit into your family.

Then, see the egg as your own physical ovum and your potential for many types of creativity, including motherhood. Send your pain as well as your hopes and dreams into this egg. Then bury it in the pot of earth (or in the ground), asking the Earth Mother to cleanse your pain and bring your dreams to fruition. Ask Her help in transferring your fertility to other areas of life that are more appropriate at this time.

Speak from your heart as you thank your parents for their unconditional love and support.

Thank and release all beings invoked and close the ritual.

Bury the egg and earth in a safe place outside.

Birth

The preparation for a birth ritual clearly takes place over the course of approximately nine months. During this time, the expectant family prepares for the arrival of the baby in many ways and on many levels. Not all pagans hold specific rituals for a birth, and those that do often combine it with the Naming. Many prefer to wait anywhere from three days to three months for a Naming ceremony. As a result, I have outlined a combined Birth-Naming ritual.

Depending on your family and the circumstances surrounding the birth, waiting can be a good idea. New parents need not feel pressured to hold a birth ritual immediately when they have a million other things to deal with and are running on a serious lack of sleep. You don't have to worry that the Gods will not recognize your child without this ceremony. Should anything happen to this child before a ceremony is performed, that child's spirit will go on with the assistance of all his or her spirits as usual. The Old Gods and Goddesses would never turn Their backs on a child simply for lack of a ritual.

Birth/Naming

Set up altar with pastel colors, flowers, candles. Spring flowers are best, if possible. Smudge or burn incense (rose, amber). Have on the altar blessing oils or water, gifts for the child, any Medicine pouches, or other sacred objects for the child. Be sure the mother and baby are comfortable and all potential needs are easily accessible, i.e. diaper change, milk, etc.

Create sacred space in your preferred manner.

The ceremonial leader invokes the chosen Gods and Goddesses, the spirit guides, and guardians of the child and his or her family, and any other beings you wish to have present. The leader states the purpose of this rite—that you have gathered to honor and celebrate the return of this being to this reality and his or her entrance into your family. Ask Their guidance and protection during this ritual and beyond, that your every action may honor them.

The ceremonial leader touches the water or oil to the child's forehead and names him/her. The leader then continues with the water or oil, blessing the child at each chakra point. You might choose to use blessings that correspond with the chakras, i.e./clarity at the third eye, love at the heart, etc.

The ceremonial leader thanks this being, _____ (child's name), on behalf of everyone present for choosing this family, for his or her presence in your lives, and for sharing his or her Earth journey.

Go around the circle (or go back and forth between mother and father if no one else is present)
three times offering personal blessings and promises
of love and/or guidance that you are committed to
give this child throughout his or her life.

The gifts are blessed and any sacred items are
charged with the intent of this celebration.

The leader (or parent, if a parent is not the
leader) takes the child to each quarter. The leader
presents the child as ____ and asks the blessings
and protection of the Spirits of the directions for
this child. The child is then held out to Father Sky,
Mother Earth, and the Great Spirit at the center.
He or she is presented as ___ and blessings are re-
quested. The parent promises to raise this child ___
in honor and to teach him/her respect for All Life.

The parent(s) once more offer their own blessings and promises to this child.

The leader thanks and releases all beings invoked and closes the ritual.

Parenthood Blessing

The following ritual is designed for the new mother
and/or father. It marks your entry into a new role as a parent and allows you a ritual space to ask for spiritual guidance and protection on this new path.

Set up altar with pastel and primary colors,
flowers, candles, symbols of mother/fatherhood,
photos of you and your child(ren). Smudge or
burn incense. Have on the altar blessing oils and
your Medicine pouches or a clear quartz crystal.

Create sacred space in your preferred manner.

Invoke your chosen Gods and Goddesses
(especially Mother or Father Deities), your spirit
guides and guardians, and any other beings you

wish to have present. Ask Their guidance and protection during this ritual and beyond, that your every action may honor them. State the purpose of this rite as a celebration and honoring of your passage into a new phase of life; mother/fatherhood. Ask the guidance of your Deities and guides in this new identity of yours.

Touch the oil or water to your own chakra points, naming yourself as Mother/Father and bless yourself with each chakra point. You may wish to invoke the Mother/Father within you and specific qualities corresponding to each chakra.

Meditate on what parenthood means to you, on the specifics of your family and how you hope to grow through this experience/what you hope to bring to your family.

Say to all you invoked and to your family members (who may or may not be present) what kind of parent you choose to be. Vow to these beings to be the best parent, teacher, student, friend, etc. that you can be and promise to remain open to spirit guidance for the greatest good of all.

Go to each quarter and present yourself as a new mother/father. Ask the blessings and protection of the Spirits of the directions on this new journey you taking. Present yourself to Father Sky, Mother Earth, and the Great Spirit at the center and ask Their continued blessings and presence along the way. Promise to be a living example of strength, balance, and love for your child(ren) and to create a family of honor and respect for All Life.

Thank and release all spirits you invoked and close the Circle.

Adulthood

The passage into adulthood is one of the most overlooked events in modern society. There are any number of reasons for this, including the fact that most people are not really sure when a child is no longer a child. Young people are not allowed to vote or enlist in the armed forces until they are eighteen. The legal age of consumption or consent varies according to the state. But once a girl begins to menstruate and a boy has his first ejaculation, they can physically become parents. In most native cultures, this is the age of adulthood and young people are treated differently as a result. They are also expected to behave with more maturity as well.

We do our children a disservice when we turn these wonderful physical events into something to be ignored or feel ashamed of. These are the physical manifestations that follow a child's readiness to be entrusted with additional responsibility and to be no longer treated as a child. Unfortunately in modern society, our children are rarely prepared for adulthood except through intellectual learning. Many are simply not ready to be treated as young adults in their early teens or before.

On the other hand, we cannot know what children are ready for unless we give them the opportunity. Puberty is a time when many children rebel. Certainly much of this is due to hormonal changes and all the confusion that comes with it, but often these children-who-are-no-longer-children need greater freedom, responsibility, and input into decisions regarding their own lives. This is part of the preparation and follow-up to the adulthood rites of passage.

In preparation for adulthood rites of passage, children should have learned and begun to demonstrate that they are willing and able to handle the responsibilities associated with being a young adult. It is your responsibility to ensure that they have been taught about the realities of sexuality, drinking and drug use, driving, and anything else that combines freedom with responsibility and potential danger.

Parents should also discuss what they know of men's and women's mysteries. This generally includes gender-specific spirituality and how to work most effectively with the Deities of your gender. It will also include more specific physical discussions, as well as discussions on interacting honorably with those of the opposite gender. If the child has indicated that they are homosexual or bisexual, there will be similar discussions on honor coupled with discussions of the unique issues facing those of alternate sexual preferences.

I know there are many single parents out there who may find it difficult at best to have these types of discussions with a child of the opposite gender. However, without a trusted adult of the same gender as the child, it is your responsibility. Hopefully, you have been able to maintain open communication and trust with your child. Keep in mind that, while a father may not really understand the Moon Lodge, he may be the ideal person to discuss sexuality and boys with his daughter. Open to spiritual guidance and trust that you will communicate what needs to be said.

Even if there is no community or family Moon Lodge for your daughter to participate in, she should be encouraged to honor her Moontime. This is something that will require support and understanding from the entire family. The Moon Lodge can be vital to your daughter's self-confidence and self-esteem. In this way, menstruation becomes a sacred time for visioning, rest, and cleansing rather than the embarrassment or annoyance it has become in modern society. Young women need to be able to reclaim their power after so many thousands of years of repression and they need to be able to do so in a balanced way.

Menarche Ritual

Set up altar with red altar cloth and symbols of the Moon, the Goddess as Maiden and Mother, your Moon blood: for example, red and white candles and flowers, a blood jar, pictures or symbols of the Moon as new and full.

Drum or sing each woman into the circle/ smudge each woman as she enters.

Create sacred space in your preferred manner.

The ceremonial leader invokes the usual or chosen Goddesses. She states the purpose of this rite—that we have gathered to honor and celebrate the entrance of_____ into the Sisterhood of Women and the Mysteries of the Blood. Ask their guidance and protection during this ritual and beyond, that your every action may honor Them.

The ceremonial leader brings the girl before the altar and instructs her in the sanctity of the Circle of Women. There is a brief discussion on strength and power of woman and the feminine energies. This is followed by one on the importance of balance in all things and of honoring the God within. The importance of honesty, community, and support among the Sisterhood is reaffirmed. The new woman is asked if she is ready for her role as a strong, creative woman and if she accepts her power, she is then presented with a special necklace, is anointed with special oils, or her face is painted with red moons. She is then blessed as a new Sister of the Blood Mysteries.

The young woman then invokes her guides, guardians, Goddesses, calling upon one in particular to work through her this night and continue to work with her in the Mysteries as she comes into her power as woman. She offers her blessings to the Sisterhood and vows to uphold the sacredness and integrity of both that Circle and herself.

She will then act as priestess and ceremonial leader for the rest of the ritual.

Meditation

Feel roots growing down from your body deep into Mother Earth. Extend your Self deep into Her center. Feel Her energy flowing up into the soles of your feet. Feel this grounding, empowering, beautiful energy flowing up filling your entire body. Breathe this energy into your entire being for a moment.

Raise your arms and send out branches into the center of Father Sky. Extend your Self into His center. Feel this expansive, empowering energy flowing down throughout your entire body. Breathe this energy into your entire being for a moment

Feel these two energies flowing through you at once. Feel them meet and merge together in your center. Feel their differences and how they balance each other. They seem to dance throughout you.

You overflow with this energy. Feel it completely surround your body. Send it out to your Sisters in Circle. Send it beyond this circle out into the Earth and the Universe. See this energy permeate all things and connect you to all of Life.

The young woman speaks of the interconnections of all life and how all our relations are sacred. She speaks from her heart of the role of women in this sacred plan and how she intends to fulfill her place in that sacred plan. She allows any messages to come through her (silently or aloud) from her special Goddess.

Go around the circle three times sharing stories of first blood and blessings for this young woman.

She is then presented with a basic red leather or cloth bag with which to construct her own Moon pouch. She is given special herbs to keep in her pouch and she blesses these now with her intentions as a sacred woman and creative force. The rest of the pouch will be completed and kept in private by her alone.

Going around the circle, each woman presents the new Sister with a gift and a secret or story about being a woman. Each woman honors her as an equal, although younger, woman and finally offers a specific promise of continuing help or support.

The new Sister of the Circle of Women honors and thanks her Sisters with renewed promises to be a living example of female strength and to uphold the integrity of this Circle. She thanks and releases all Goddesses, guides, and guardians invoked and then closes the ritual.

Manhood

It is just as important for our young men to claim their power in healthy and balanced ways. Over the last two thousand years or so, the natural creativity, intuition, sensitivity, and nurturing abilities of men have been repressed. They need to know that protection and strength need not preclude integrity and love.

Menstruating women are automatically in a perfect space for visioning each month. While women may certainly seek visions at other time, the vision quests of many cultures were designed to bring men to that same place of psychic receptivity and altered states. This is excellent preparation for a young man before his rite of passage, even if his vision quest must take place in your backyard.

Set up altar with dark blue or dark green altar cloth and symbols of the Sun, the God, and your helping spirits.

Drum each man into the circle/smudge each man as he enters.

Create sacred space in your preferred manner.

The ceremonial leader invokes the chosen Gods. He states the purpose of this rite—that you have gathered to honor and celebrate the entrance of_____ into the Brotherhood of Men. Ask their guidance and protection during this ritual and beyond, that your every action may honor them.

The ceremonial leader brings the young man before the altar and instructs him in the sanctity of Circle and the honor in the bonds between men. There is a brief discussion on strength and power of man and the masculine energies.

This is followed by one on the importance of balance in all things and of honoring the Goddess within. The importance of honesty, community, and support among the Brotherhood is reaffirmed. The young man is asked if he is ready for his role as a strong, sensitive man and if he accepts his power. He is then presented with a special necklace, is anointed with special oils, or his body is painted with symbols of the God, creativity, strength, fertility, etc. He is then blessed as a new member of the Brotherhood of Men.

The young man invokes his guides, guardians, and Gods, calling upon one in particular to work through him this night and continue to work with him in the Mysteries as he comes into his power as a man. He offers his blessings to the Brotherhood and vows to protect and uphold the sacredness and integrity of himself and the Brotherhood.

He will then act as priest and ceremonial leader for the rest of the ritual.

Meditation

You are running through a forest. Faster and faster you run, feeling the strength and vitality of your body as you speed through the woods. You stop as you come to a clearing. In the center of the clearing is a huge man. He calls you to come to him. As you approach, he seems to shift his shape. You cannot tell whether he is human or animal.

Although he is a frightening sight, you continue to approach him. As you do, he grabs you by the shoulders and looks deep into your eyes. He probes your very soul as he asks you if you are ready to be a man. Answer him honestly and allow any emotion you may feel to flow forth.

As you stare into his eyes, you are pulled into his being. Within him, you experience tremendous strength. You know it is your responsibility to protect your loved ones. You look deeper and realize that it is also your responsibility to protect all beings and the Earth Herself.

Looking deeper, you hold a baby, then an injured deer with the greatest tenderness you have ever known. You realize that love and gentleness are strengths, too.

Looking even deeper, you see the Goddess. She embraces you, and you realize that you and She are One. You realize that balance is necessary in all things.

Suddenly, you are standing before the huge man, and he no longer frightens you. He kisses on the forehead and tells you how proud he is of you. Listen for any other messages he may have for you before returning to your body and the Circle.

The young man speaks of the interconnections of all life and how all our relations are sacred. He speaks from his heart of the role of men in this

239

sacred plan and how he intends to fulfill his place in that sacred plan. He allows any messages to come through him (silently or aloud) from his special God. If he feels it is appropriate, he may share his experience of the meditation.

Going around the circle, each man presents the new Brother with a gift and a secret or story about being a man. Each man honors him as an equal, although newer, member of the Brotherhood and finally offers a specific promise of continuing help or support for him.

He then honors and thanks his Brothers with renewed promises to be a living example of male strength and to uphold the integrity of the Brotherhood. He thanks and releases all Gods, guides, and guardians invoked and then closes the ritual.

Dedication

If you follow a specific tradition, it is very likely that this ritual will be spelled out for you. However, most pagans today do not follow a definite and established magical system. It is for you that I have outlined a dedication ritual. This ritual should only be performed when children have attained a basic level of understanding of the family path and have decided that this is their path. It is written as a solo ritual, but parents may participate as ritual support, guides, and Circle guardians.

Use your personal altar with symbols of your personal helping spirits and the Deities you feel close to. Smudge or burn incense. Have blessing oil or water ready.

Create sacred space in your preferred manner.

Invoke your chosen Gods and Goddesses, your spirit guides, and any other beings you wish to have present. State the purpose of this rite: that you are here to dedicate yourself to your chosen path and to the Gods of that path. Ask the guidance and protection of those invoked during this ritual and beyond, that your every action may honor Them.

Sit in silent meditation for a few moments, reviewing what you know of this path and what led to your decision to follow this path. Be certain of your decision before moving ahead with the ritual.

Take up the blessing oil or water and hold it between both hands. Offer it to those invoked and ask for their blessings.

Anoint yourself with the oil or water, blessing yourself with the qualities you want to bring to this path. You may choose to anoint each chakra point with blessings specific to that chakra.

Stand before each quarter, saying that you dedicate yourself to this path and to the spirits and Deities of this path. Ask for their blessings and their guidance. Promise to live your life with honesty and integrity, honoring the spirits with your every action. Then present yourself to Father Sky, Mother Earth, and the Great Spirit or the God and Goddess at the center of the Circle. Ask for Their blessings and Their guidance. Promise to live your life with honesty and integrity, honoring Them with your every action.

Thank and release all beings invoked and close the ritual.

Death

The issue of death is a complex one that cannot be covered in one section or even one chapter. However, death does affect children, and it is important to deal with in this book. In chapter 7, I discussed how to handle the questions that will inevitably arise regarding death. In this chapter, there are some very specific aspects of guiding children through the death of a loved one that I would like to address.

The loss of a child strikes a heartbreaking, protective chord in most of us. The mere idea of a suffering child can send the media and society into a frenzy of anger and righteous indignation. For a parent, the loss of a child can be devastating. Most parents have a deeply ingrained resistance even to the thought of losing a child as a possibility.

One Wiccan woman I knew many years ago held an entire ritual for herself after the loss of her child. She used a perfect, unopened rose and a crystal egg to symbolize her child's innate beauty and unrealized potential. She called upon the Mother Goddesses to aid her in her grief and help her to find ways to go on living. At the conclusion of her Circle, she buried the rose and the crystal deep within the Earth. In doing this, she commended the body and spirit of her child to the Great Mother. She prayed to the Mother of All, asking that She carry her child's spirit to the next world with the enveloping love of a mother for her own child. As a mother myself, this beautifully simple ritual brings tears to my eyes.

Death rites of passage serve to bring closure and healing to both the living and dead. Well-constructed memorial services are designed to encourage the living to grieve openly and to provide a safe forum for them to do so. It is vital that children are allowed to grieve and to do so in their own ways.

In guiding children through the process of death and grief, parents must be careful not to tell them how to feel or how to act. There is no "right" way to grieve, and children, like all of us, must find their own way. In this situation, a parent must become a guide and counselor, encouraging children to talk about it, helping them to sort out their feelings, and allowing them privacy when they need it.

Since children may not always be able to verbalize exactly what they are feeling, it is often up to parents to come up with creative ways to help them stay connected to their inner selves. Working with the water element can be a powerful means of preventing the blockages that can occur as the result of emotional trauma. Utilizing some form of creative outlet, such as music, maskmaking, or sculpture, is also recommended as is making the most of physical release through sports or play.

Because of their natural creativity, children can gain even more comfort and closure from rituals than adults do. Rites of passage speak to them from the depths of their hearts and imaginations. Including children in the planning of these ceremonies provides them with the opportunity to do something concrete for the departed loved one and for themselves. This allows children a vital feeling of inclusion, which is often lacking for them at times like this.

Due to their relative lack of energy filters and their readiness to trust, children are often open to communications from spirit guidance and departed loved ones. Trusting in their intuitive suggestions for rituals can result in a simple, yet truly profound ceremony. They often have a way of innately knowing at a heart level, what is needed by those around them.

The death of a pet can affect a child very deeply. To most pagan families, pets are part of the family, and we feel their passage as strongly as the death of most human loved ones. As family members, they deserve to have their own memorial services or funerals. This is a time for us to honor them and to say goodbye. It can be a safe forum from which to tell them how much they mean to us and to release their spirits lovingly.

It is unfortunate that the death of a pet is often ignored by the majority culture. People who react strongly to this type of death are often perceived as silly, weak, or just plain ridiculous. It is very important that pagan parents treat the death of a pet in the same manner as the death of a beloved human, particularly if your children were close to the animal. They may not be our physical children, but we often feel that they are our spiritual children. Furthermore, our children may bond to these animals as though they are siblings, especially young children.

Since death rituals for animals are generally handled as private family affairs, and there are not many books available detailing how to perform these, I have outlined two rituals for you to use as a guide.

Burial Ritual for an Animal

Using incense, smudge, or a drum, purify the area and charge it with healing energy. If this animal disliked fire or smoke, omit those elements.

Once the grave has been dug, place some flowers or herbs in the base. You might choose to use Forget-Me-Nots, roses, or other flowers you associate with everlasting love. Some beneficial herbs are: sandalwood for its high spiritual energies or true sage (*Salvia* spp.) for its association with immortality, healing, and protection. Then place the body on top of these, and cover it with a few more of the flowers or herbs.

If you have chosen to place personal items, crystals, or other stones in the grave now is the time to charge them (if this has not already been done) with energy and place them in with the body.

Call upon the Spirits of the directions, the God, and the Goddess to join with you in this ceremony. Ask that They bless your work. Request guidance, that your every action may honor Them.

Call upon the spirit of the departed to join with you in this ceremony.

Offer a prayer, such as: "Through this ceremony, we commend the body of our beloved ____ to the Earth as we entrust this spirit to the Lord and Lady. We gather here to honor our beloved and to send our blessings for a joyous reunion with the Creator."

The leader leads the gathering in a special prayer or song at this point. I would recommend that this focus on the continuity of life and love as well as celebrate life, freedom, and rebirth.

If one person has been designated to replace the earth in the grave, do so now. Alternatively, you may choose to take turns each placing a shovel full of earth in the grave. However you choose to organize this, make each step a sacred one.

With each consecutive shovel-full, offer a prayer to the Earth who receives this body, to the being who is now on his way to a new life, and to the Great Spirit, God, or Goddess who will receive his spirit. Continue to offer prayers for peace, love, release, and anything else you choose, until the grave is full.

Holding hands and forming a circle, if you can, sit or stand around the grave. Allow yourself to feel every emotion you experience. Feel comfortable expressing these emotions as an offering of honesty and respect for this departed animal.

Go around the circle and take turns offering prayers, good wishes, stories, jokes, and whatever you feel. Continue this until all present feel some sense of release.

Offer one final prayer. "Although we grieve for the times we will no longer share in this world, we rejoice in your freedom. We are grateful for the sharing of our lives during your time here in this world. Your memories and gifts live on within each of us as we freely release you to your next world. We send you heartfelt blessings of peace, love, and joy. We say not good-bye, but farewell until we meet again."

Memorial Service for an Animal

This may also be used as part of an ashes-scattering ceremony after a cremation. If you know that this animal disliked smudge or smoke, omit those elements unless this ceremony takes place at least one month after the animal's death.

Prepare the area with any flowers or decorations you prefer. Set up a simple altar with a photo of the departed in the center, surrounded by personal effects and items symbolizing the Earth and Great Spirit or God and Goddess.

Using incense, smudge, or a drum, purify the area. Charge it with healing and loving energy.

Set up a central altar on a blanket inside or outside—at the animal's favorite spot. Place a picture of the animal in the center and surround it with items that were special to this animal or items that are symbolic of this animal's favorite things, places, and people. Also on this blanket, have a bowl of earth. As is true with the human rite, the earth is our Earth Mother to whom this animal's body has returned.

Clear those attending with your drum or smudge as they enter. The ritual leader should explain the symbolism of the altar and other decorations to those attending. Allow everyone some time to look over the altar and get comfortable.

Sit or stand in a circle. The leader states the purpose for this ritual and invites the spirit of the animal to join in. Any other Deities or spirits you wish to invite should be called at this time.

Go around the circle, speaking your prayers for this animal. Share stories and feelings about your time together or your grief. Everyone should be made comfortable to say what they feel. Go

around the circle at least three times until everyone feels some sense of release and closure.

Ground and center in your preferred manner, if
necessary.

Conclude with specific prayers and blessings of
release, peace, and love. Allow everyone time to
let this animal know how honored they were to
have shared this life, how grateful they are for the
blessings of that relationship, and how much they
will always love that animal. Encourage everyone
present to release their ties to this animal so that
she or he may easily move onto the next world.

Some families will choose to honor this animal's
memory by giving a home to another animal in
need. If this is the case, let the departed animal
know that this is what you have chosen to do and
ask for his or her blessing in this. Promise to honor
and love the new animal as family, yet make it
clear that no one will ever replace this departed
animal in your hearts.

Finish up by doing something that may have
been special to this animal. If this animal loved to
hike in a particular place, go there for a walk; if
this animal tended to be a couch potato, lie around
all day. Be aware during this time of the possibility that this animal may decide to be with you.

I would like to end this chapter with the following ceremony to create a special Medicine bundle or altar to the
memory of the departed, whether human or animal. This
can be extremely beneficial in the acknowledgement of the
time it may take for us to release our bonds to the departed
completely and to heal from these wounds. It offers both
children and adults a concrete method of hanging on and
gradually releasing the departed loved one when they are
ready. This brings an element of control back into the

situation in that you do not need to release the altar or bundle until you decide to.

This is a common process among indigenous peoples for the remembering and gradual easing of grief. Generally speaking, these altars or bundles are kept and honored for one year after the death of the loved one. At the end of that year, the honored items are ceremonially either burned or buried in recognition of the end of a mourning period and to release the loved one fully to the next world.

Creation of a Memorial Altar or Medicine Bundle

If this ceremony is for an individual that disliked smudge or smoke, omit those elements unless this ceremony takes place at least one month after the death.

Select the items you wish to include in this altar or Medicine bundle. These may include a lock of hair, a photo, items that were special to the departed, and anything else that you feel is important, including any symbols relating to the spirit guides of the departed. If you have chosen to create a Medicine bundle, also select the bag or cloth to be used to contain the bundle items.

Put together and bind your Medicine bundle or set up the altar.

Purify the ritual space and all ritual items, using either the smudge ceremony or the drum purification ceremony.

When purifying any leather or other animal parts to be used in the construction of the altar or bundle, be sure to release and honor the spirits of these animals. Thank them for the gifts of their bodies and make an offering to their spirits of some kind. This may be anything from a donation to a wildlife refuge to a direct offering of food or water.

Call upon the Spirits of the directions, the God, and the Goddess or the Great Spirit to join with you in this ceremony. Ask that They bless your work. Request guidance, that your every action may honor Them.

Call upon the spirit of the departed to join with you in this honoring ceremony.

Holding your hands out over the items to be used, bless them with the memory of your departed loved one. "This altar/bundle will be honored as the symbolic representative of ___. Through this altar/bundle, we maintain a physical connection to you and you continue to share a physical space within our home. This altar/bundle will be an instrument of love and healing for all of us and will be ceremonially released when we no longer need its energy."

"In creating this altar/bundle, we acknowledge that we have not yet released all ties to our departed ___. We ask the blessings of the God and the Goddess or the Great Spirit and all our spirit guides in our time of grief and healing. Guide us that we may fully heal and rejoice in this glorious transition."

Thank all those spirits who joined with you in this work, particularly the departed, spirit guides, and the God and the Goddess or the Great Spirit. Release them and let them know they are always welcome at your home.

*At the end of the year, or whenever you feel the time is right, you will ceremonially bury or burn these items. The burial ritual given above may be easily altered for this purpose. This basic outline can also be used for a burning. Rather than commending the altar/bundle to the Earth, you will ask that the fire purify and cleanse your grief and anything still binding this spirit to our world. Request that the spirit of your loved one be released by the fire and that the smoke carry him or her directly to the God and the Goddess or the Great Spirit.

Chapter 13
Our Future

Pagan parents are pioneers in many ways. As pagans, we are living a healthy and growing spiritual tradition with great potential for all of us. As parents, we have the opportunity to lead the way in raising happy, healthy, connected children. Much of modern society is sadly lacking in respect, honor, and community, and we can begin to return that to our reality, through how we live our lives and how we raise our children.

Our children truly are our future. Not only do they carry on our genes and family names, but they also will be the ones to develop modern paganism and continue the Ancient Ways in their lives. How they are raised plays an important role in who they become. As parents, we can choose to raise wounded kids who conform to the current mainstream culture or we can do our best to create an environment that supports them in healthy, loving, and spiritual ways.

Pagan parents are working toward creating healthy community and keeping true spirituality alive in our world—even if only within our families. We are doing all we can to raise conscious children who have a better chance to avoid the trap of modern commercialism and modern "progress."

God is not dead to pagans. Nor is the Goddess. We feel Them everywhere. They are the trees, the rocks, the buildings, the other people. They are Us, and we recognize that. They are our children, and we must treat them as such. We teach our children, through word and action, that when we respect the Earth and other beings, we respect ourselves and everyone wins.

Pagan parents have the opportunity to guide a new generation back into a more sacred way of living on this Earth. When we walk in balance and with integrity, we become powerful examples of strength and sensitivity, power and grace. And when we combine that with complete, unconditional love and play, we open the doors to truly beautiful relationships with our children. We become the parents we always wanted, and always dreamed of being.

This is the hope of our world. As parents, we are in a unique position to contribute to the future of our world and our families. Only through self-awareness and living with integrity can we hope to give our children the tools to create a preferred reality. As pagan parents, I know we are all working and praying toward that end.

Now this sounds like a huge responsibility—and it is. But it need not be intimidating. If you are a new parent, don't worry that you will do it wrong. As a pagan or heathen parent reading this book, you have already shown that you are not willing to live your life on automatic and do the least amount of work to get you through. You are exploring, researching, and bringing the Gods into your life and your role as a parent.

The best way to handle this responsibility is to be you! Trust your love for your family and your connections to your spirit allies. Don't try to take it all on by yourself. Work with the exercises in this book and keep up your personal spiritual practice. Be honest with yourself and your family and work with them, and the spirits, to co-create a beautiful reality for all of you. And remember, there are plenty of other pagan and heathen parents out here going through similar things. Call on us for support, advice, or just someone to vent to.

I thank you for your part in creating out future. It is an honor to share the title of *Pagan Parent* with all of you. I love our diversity and the way that we truly and deeply love our kids. And I feel so blessed that there are so many other pagan kids with parents like you that our son will meet and create pagan community with for years to come.

Many Blessings for You and Yours!

Contacts

General

Circle Network News
    PO Box 219, Mt. Horeb, WI 53572
    www.circlesanctuary.org
    Email circle@mhtc.net

Covenant of Unitarian Universalist Pagans
    8190A Beechmont Avenue #335, Cincinnati, OH
        45255-3154
    www.cuups.org   Email CUUPS@aol.com

Military Pagan Network
    P.O. Box 253
    Ellicott City, MD 21041-0253 telephone (410)750-3327
    John Machate, Coordinator/CEO
    www.milpagan.org/   Email coordinator@milpagan.org

Pagan Educational Network
    PO Box 1364, Bloomington, IN 47402-1364
    [please send business-sized SASE for mail requests]
    www.bloomington.in.us/~pen/
    Email pen@bloomington.in.us

Order of Bards, Ovates, and Druids
   PO Box 1333, Lewes, East Sussex, BN7 1DX, England
   www.druidry.org   Email office@obod.co.uk

Legal Resources

American Civil Liberties Union
   ACLU, 125 Broad Street, 18th Floor, New York,
      New York 10004-2400
   www.aclu.org

Americans United for the Separation of Church and State
   www.au.org

Earth Religions Legal Assistance Network
   www.conjure.com/ERAL/eral.html

Lady Liberty League (LLL)
   PO Box 219, Mt. Horeb, WI 53572
   www.circlesanctuary.org/liberty/
   circle@mhtc.net
   (608) 924-2216   FAX (608) 924-5961

Military Pagan Network
   Military Pagan Network Inc.
   Dept. of Harassment Affairs,
   Director: Stephenie Urquhart
   1634 Moran Rd, Choctaw, OK 73020
   www.milpagan.org/

Ontario Consultants on Religious Tolerance
   US Postal Address:
   OCRT, PO Box 514, Wellesley Island, NY 13640-0514
   Canadian Postal Address:
   OCRT, Box 27026, Frontenac PO, Kingston ON
      Canada K7M 8W5

Email: ocrt_qu@cgo.wave.ca
Fax: (613) 531-9609

United States Constitution
www.law.cornell.edu/constitution/
constitution.overview.html

U.S. Bill of Rights
www.law.cornell.edu/constitution/
constitution.billofrights.html

Witches League for Public Awareness
WLPA P.O. Box 909, Rehoboth, Massachusetts 02769
www.CelticCrow.com/
Email hernesson@aol.com

Witches Voice
The Witches' Voice Inc., P.O. Box 4924, Clearwater,
Florida 33758-4924
telephone (813) 723-0734 (press Star button for fax)
www.witchvox.com
Email WebMaster@witchvox.com

Recommended Reading

General Health and Healing

The Anatomy Coloring Book by Wynn Kapit and Lawrence
    M. Elson. Canfield Press.
How to Raise a Healthy Child...In Spite of Your Doctor by
Robert S. Mendelsohn, M.D. Ballantine Books.
Smart Medicine for a Healthier Child by Janet Zand, Lac.,
    O.M.D.; Rachel Walton, R.N.; and Bob Rountree,
    M.D. Avery Publishing Group.

Healing Stones

Color and Crystals by Joy Gardner. The Crossing Press.
Love is in the Earth: A Kaleidoscope of Crystals by Melody.
    Earth-Love Publishing House.
The Women's Book of Healing by Diane Stein. Llewellyn
    Publications.

Homeopathy

Homeopathy for Pregnancy, Birth, and Your Baby's First
    Year by Miranda Castro. St. Martin's Press.
Homeopathic Medicine at Home by Maesimond B. Panos,
    M.D. and Jane Heimlich. Jeremy P. Tarcher, Inc.

Herbs

Natural Healing with Herbs by Humbart Santillo, B.S., M.H. Hohm Press

Wise Woman Herbal for the Childbearing Year by Susun S. Weed. Ash Tree Publishing.

Body Work

Chinese Pediatric Massage Therapy by Ya-li Fan. Blue Poppy Press.

Infant Massage by Vimala Schneider McClure. Bantam Books.

Kundalini Yoga for Strength, Success, & Spirit by Ravi Singh. White Lion Press.

Shiatsu Therapy: Theory and Practice by Toru Namikoshi. Japan Publications, Inc.

Diet & Nutrition

The Complete New Guide to Preparing Baby Foods by Sue Castle. Bantam Books.

The Low Blood Sugar Handbook by Edward & Patricia Krimmel. Franklin Publishers.

The Self-Healing Cookbook by Kristina Turner. Earthtones Press.

Sugar Busters! by H. Leighton Steward; Morrison C. Bethea, M.D.; Sam S. Andrews, M.D.; Luis A. Balart, M.D. Ballantine Books.

Vegetarian Mother Baby Book by Rose Elliot. Pantheon Books.

Energy Work

The Energy Within by Richard M. Chin, M.D., O.M.D. Paragon House.

Hands of Light by Barbara Brennan. Bantam Books.

Reiki: Universal Life Energy by Bodo J. Baginski and Shalila Sharamon. Life Rhythm Publications

Wheels of Light by Rosalyn L Bruyere. Simon & Schuster.

Breathing

Science of Breath by Swami Rama, Rudolph Ballentine, M.D., and Alan Hymes, M.D. Himalayan International Institute of Yoga Science and Philosophy.

Pagan Paths

Celebrating the Great Mother by Cait Johnson and Maura D. Shaw. Destiny Books.

Circle Round by Starhawk and Diane Baker and Anne Hill. Bantam Doubleday Dell Publishers.

New Moon Rising: Reclaiming the Sacred Rites of Menstruation by Linda Heron Wind. Delphi Press.

Pagan Homeschooling by Kristin Madden. Spilled Candy Publications

Pagan Kids' Activity Book by Amber K. Horned Owl Publishing

Raising Witches by Ashleen O'Gaea. New Page Books

Wheel of the Year by Pauline Campanelli. Llewellyn Publications.

Wild Girls: The Path of the Young Goddess by Patricia Monaghan. Llewellyn Publications.

Death and Dying

The Pagan Book of Living and Dying by Starhawk, M. Macha Nightmare, and the Reclaiming Collective. HarperSanFrancisco Publishers.

On Children and Death by Elisabeth Kubler-Ross, M.D. Simon & Schuster.

Bereaved Children and Teens edited by Earl A. Grollman. Beacon Press.

Sleep Issues

The Family Bed by Tine Thevenin. Avery Publishing Group, Inc.

Helping Your Child Sleep Through The Night by Joanne Cuthbertson and Susie Schevill. Doubleday.

Solve Your Child's Sleep Problems by Richard Ferber, M.D.

Parenting and Discipline

How to Keep Your Kids from Driving You Crazy by Paula
Stone Bender, Ph.D. John Wiley & Sons, Inc.

Time-Out For Toddlers by Dr. James W. Varni and Donna
G. Corwin. Berkley Books.

The Strong-Willed Child by Dr. James Dobson.   Living
Books.

Magazines

The Blessed Bee, PO Box 641, Point Arena, CA 95468
Subscription $13
www.blessedbee.com
or call 888-724-3966

Acorns Newsletter (Pagan Homeschooling and Parenting)
393 Arbor Lane, Prattville Alabama 36066
Free email newsletter; print subscription $14.99
www.paganchildren.com/acorns.htm

Glossary

Asatru: the worship of the Nordic pantheon; roughly translated as "belief in the Old Gods."

Astral Body: the spirit or energetic double that travels freely during trance states and dreaming

Astral Travel: to travel in spirit only without the physical body

Aura: the personal energy field; that which permeates and surrounds the physical body

Body soul: A shamanic term for that part of the spirit of personal energy field that remains with the physical body as long as it lives.

Chakra: an energy vortex or center of activity for the subtle, life force that permeates and animates the physical body. They are believed to be interrelated with the parasympathetic, sympathetic, and autonomic nervous systems.

Deathwalk: the psychopompic shamanic journey after physical death into the next World.

Deathwalker: a shaman who deals with the dying and the dead; a psychopomp: one who guides the departed beyond this life into the next world and/or connects them with their spirit guides after death.

Devas: Nature fairies, generally seen as very small and often amorphous.

Empathic: one who psychically receives the feelings and emotions of other people.

Empathetic: one who can understand or relate to the way another feels.

Free soul: a shamanic term for the astral body

Hologram: a three-dimensional image; each piece of the hologram contains the image of
the whole.

Homeopathy: a system of healing based on the concept of "like cures like."

Hundredth-Monkey phenomenon: referring to the book by the same name, "the hundredth monkey" by Ken Keyes. The idea is that once a certain critical percentage of a population has learned or developed an ability, the remainder of that population will instantly (or "overnight") develop the same ability.

Incarnation: the process of entering physical form; rebirth

Kundalini: generally dormant energy that is said to reside at the base of the spine. It is often compared to a sleeping serpent. It is a vital energy, both static and kinetic, that is one's power; one's fire of enlightenment and awakening.

Nagual: the mysterious, Otherworldly aspect of Self.

Norse: referring to the Nordic or Scandinavian peoples.

Polyamoury: non-monogamous

Psychometry: the ability to obtain psychic impressions from inanimate objects.

Quickening: The time when a pregnant woman first feels the movement of her baby; usually occurring around four months of pregnancy.

Saami: the indigenous people of northern Norway, Sweden, Finland, and the Russian Kola Peninsula; commonly known as Lapps or Laplanders.

Santeria: based on the beliefs of the Yoruban peoples who were brought to the Americas as slaves. Santo means saint and refers to the African Gods that were assimilated as Christian saints.

Santero: a practitioner of the Santeria religion; usually male; Santera usually denotes a female practitioner.

Scrying: a method of divination using a glass or bowl of water as a focal point.

Shamanism: an ancient spiritual path characterized by the shamanic journey, or conscious and controlled astral travel.

Sidhe: the Great Elves or Fairy folk of the ancient Celts; generally seen as human size or larger and very powerful.

Soul fragmentation: the energetic blocks or loss of energy and memories that result from trauma.

Soul retrieval: a shamanic process to retrieve and reintegrate lost and blocked soul fragments.

Spirit Guides: any interdimensional beings that teach, guide and guard humans.

Telepathy: wordless, psychic communication.

Thoughtform: a psychic creation that has form and, with enough energy, may develop a life of its own.

Tonal: the rational, everyday aspect of Self.

Universal energy field: the energy or Spirit that permeates and connects all things in all worlds.

Voudoun: also referred to as Vodou or Vaudoun; synchretized religion combining aspects of indigenous West African and Haitian beliefs with Catholicism.

Index

Index

Index

First of Its Kind

Pagan Homeschooling:
A Guide to Adding Spirituality
To Your Child's Education
By Kristin Madden

ISBN 1-892718-42-1
Trade paperback, 300 pages

Why are so many families educating their children at home?

Is this path right for you and your family? How do you get started? How can you better teach your children about your spirituality? Can spirituality and academics ever meet?

The answers to these questions and many more can be found in the pages of this groundbreaking book. The home education movement is growing at an astounding pace. Pagans and other metaphysical parents are enthusiastically exploring this option to typical compulsory school education.

Pagan Homeschooling is the first book to address the needs of these families, and this hands-on manual is *packed* with resources, checklists, questionnaires, exercises, arts and crafts, experiments, spells, rituals, and more. Here's what this book can help you do—

- Decide if home education is right for your family
- Discover your children's unique learning styles
- Hear how and why other pagan home educators are teaching their children at home
- Find out how working parents are creating ways to successfully home educate their children
- See how easy and beneficial it can be to home educate gifted and special needs children
- Learn to supplement a child's public education and incorporate spirituality in holistic ways
- Develop the ability to be a great networker
- Create effective unit studies
- Learn with the elements and festivals
- Gain access to a huge variety of educational and legal resources
- Develop your psychic and magickal abilities through School and Moon magicks
- Explore arts, crafts, history, and science with a spiritual twist

An Imaginative Fairytale for All Ages

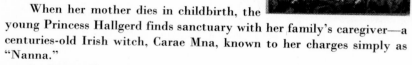

Pelzmantel:
A Medieval Tale
By K. A. Laity

ISBN 1-892718-46-4
Trade paperback, 216 pages

When her mother dies in childbirth, the young Princess Hallgerd finds sanctuary with her family's caregiver—a centuries-old Irish witch, Carae Mna, known to her charges simply as "Nanna."

In this retelling of the Grimm Brothers' tale "Allerleirau," Hallgerd grows up in exile under the witch's tutelage while the realm stagnates in the hands of her grieving father, who has come to be under the control of Thomas, a mage from Nanna's homeland.

The story is told from Nanna's point of view, allowing her to weave many other tales into the telling of Hallgerd adventures. The narrative is infused with actual stories from medieval Ireland and Scandinavia as well as inventions nonetheless firmly rounded in the author's thorough knowledge of the time period.

Medieval magick plays a major role, from genuine herbal cures to complex prognostications about the dangers facing the young royal. The focus throughout the novel remains on women's experiences in the medieval world, revealing the complexity and richness of this less well-known sphere.

> **An engaging read from a writer who, as a Ph.D. candidate in Medieval studies and a Pagan herself, knows her stuff.**
>
> **—*The Beltane Papers***

> **Laity's fast-paced book is a pleasure to read, and it will truly entertain those from age 12 to 112.**
>
> **— *New World Finn* magazine**

Stories for the Pagan Child
(and Child at Heart)

If Mermaids Could Dance:
19 Original Tales & Myths about Faer-
ies, Witches, & Goddesses,
Plus Spells
By Lady Lilith

ISBN 1-892718-51-0
Trade paperback, 156 pages

"This is a delightful treasury of original tales and myths where Faeries, Mermaids, Goddesses, and Witches live in harmony with the elements of Nature, the ways of magick, and the mysterious workings of fate. Woven throughout *If Mermaids Could Dance* by Lady Lilith are timeless stories, legends, and Witchcraft lore. One can almost hear Lady's gentle voice as the narrator unveils each fascinating story, bringing alive with carefully descriptive language the interplay of enchanted characters creating a colorful backdrop for our imaginations.

"Included in each chapter are easy instructions for us to experience that part of ourselves that always has and always will believe in the powers of magick.

"You will find this book a pleasure to read and you will want to read it aloud to your children and they to their children, keeping the Old Ways alive for generations to come."

— *Gypsy.* "Enchantress" recording artist

Lady's wisdom is a cherished thing. Read her words and remember.

— *Laurie Cabot*

This inspirational and enchanting book will lift your spirit and inspire you to pursue and achieve the goals that you have put on hold in the recesses of your mind.

— *Bucks County Herald* review

Spiritual Teachings
Disguised as Fiction

The Temple of the Twelve:
Novice of Colors
By Esmerelda Little Flame

ISBN 1-892718-32-4
Trade paperback, 284 pages

"This book had a powerful transformative effect in me spiritually," says Freya Aswynn, the acclaimed author of *Northern Mysteries & Magick* and one of the foremost authorities on runes. "I think it is in the same league as *The Celestine Prophecy*.

"The twelve chapters form Path Workings easy to visualize due to the vivid imagery used by the author. In using colors as Deities of Initiation, the author transcends all differences between the various paths of Pagan spirituality and unifies them all. I don't need Runes to predict that Esmerelda Little Flame has a great future as a spiritual writer. This book contains deep Mystery Teachings so desperately needed in the New Aeon. I will never look upon colors in the same way."

> [Esmerelda Little Flame's] prose is music to the mind...a whimsical tapestry of warmth and delight.
> —Silver Ravenwolf, *To Ride A Silver Broomstick*

What Readers Say:

I can count on one hand the number of books that have drawn me in so totally that I couldn't force myself to put them down till the end, and *The Temple of the Twelve* has been added to this list. My 13-year-old daughter is always asking me to help her learn my ways and beliefs, and I will definitely be giving her this book to read. It not only provokes thought, but it will be a wonderful tool to provoke conversation between us and aid both of us on our paths.

—**Timbermoon**

As a parent of five and an active member in the Pagan community, I plan to take these lessons to heart and try my best to pass the lessons of the colors on to our future in projects and meditations. A complete book of inspiration! This book is an excellent learning and teaching tool.

—**Hawthorn Circle**

Upcoming Books

*The Earth Child's
Handbook:
Crafts & Inspiration
for the Spiritual Child*

By Brigid Ashwood
(formerly
Brigid Smallwood)

**And from our
Re-Published Treasures line, watch for long-
forgotten stories suitable for spiritual children
and young teens, including:**

- *The Book of Nature Stories*
- *Home Animals*
- *The Stories Mother Nature
   Told Her Children*
- *Mother Nature Stories: A Book of the Best
   Nature Stories that Mothers Can Tell Their
   Children*
- *Fairy Tales of All Nations*
- *Myths and Legends of the North American
   Indians*

Read It Free, Read It Now

A Reverence for Trees:
A Love Story
By Lorna Tedder

Ebook Format only (pdf)

Lorna Tedder's short read was originally published by Berkley Publishing Company in 2002 in
the *Words of the Witches* anthology and is the first
of Spilled Candy's Re-Published Treasures series.

For more metaphysical fiction as well as non-fiction guides, visit us online at www.spilledcandy.com. Our website features articles, tips, pictures, artwork, interviews, and lots of freebies.

Some of Spilled Candy's current and upcoming books include:

- *Hidden Passages: Tales to Honor the Crones* by Vila Spiderhawk
- *The Earth Child's Handbook* by Brigid (Smallwood) Ashwood
- *Dream of the Circle of Women* by Dahti Blanchard
- *Coven of the August Moon* by Agona Darkeagle
- *Once Upon a Beltane Eve* by Selene Silverwind
- *Pagan Homeschooling* by Kristin Madden
- *If Mermaids Could Dance* by Lady Lilith
- *The Astral Grail* by D. Jason Cooper
- *Field of Jonquils* by Selene Silverwind
- *Ring of Fire* by Marline Haleff
- *Flying by Night* by Lorna Tedder
- *A Witch's Diary* by Lady Lilith
- *Access* by Lorna Tedder
- *The Wild God* by Gail Wood
- *Pelzmantel* by K. A. Laity
- *Witch Moon Rising, Witch Moon Waning* by Maggie Shayne and Lorna Tedder
- *Embracing the Goddess* by Talitha Dragonfly
- *Gift of the Dreamtime* by S. Kelley Harrell
- *The Temple of the Twelve* by Esmerelda Little Flame
- *Pagan Parenting* by Kristin Madden
- *How to Open and Run a Pagan Shop* by Terri Paajanen

Printed in the United States
21969LVS00005B/106